THE BOOK ON CAREER LEADERSHIP COACHING TODAY

Empowering Leaders to Maximize Strengths and Talents to Excel!

Lady Doris Choto

10-10-10
Publishing

The Book on Career Leadership Coaching Today: Empowering Leaders to Maximize Strengths and Talents to Excel!

ISBN: 979-8762454636

Limits of Liability and Disclaimer of Warranty
The author and publisher shall not be liable for your misuse of the enclosed material. This book is strictly for informational and educational purposes only.

Warning – Disclaimer
The purpose of this book is to educate and entertain. The author and/or publisher do not guarantee that anyone following these techniques, suggestions, tips, ideas, or strategies will become successful. The author and/or publisher shall have neither liability nor responsibility to anyone with respect to any loss or damage caused, or alleged to be caused, directly or indirectly by the information contained in this book.

Medical Disclaimer
The medical or health information in this book is provided as an information resource only, and is not to be used or relied on for any diagnostic or treatment purposes. This information is not intended to be patient education, does not create any patient-physician relationship, and should not be used as a substitute for professional diagnosis and treatment.

Publisher
10-10-10 Publishing
Canada

Printed in Canada and the United States of America

www.CareerLeadershipCoachingToday.com

Table of Contents

Dedication

You hold the keys to your career leadership journey
as a woman, man, mother, father, or student,
in whatever career or business you are involved in.

I dedicate this book to all women, men,
and children in the world. To my mother and father,
for their love and support.

To all my loved ones, who have prayed for me
and encouraged me throughout my life.

To Roger, you are an inspiration and encourager.

And finally, I dedicate this book to *you*,
the leader opening it with curiosity, open-mindedness,
and enthusiasm to sharpen your leadership,
coaching, and mentoring skills in today's
internet-based and disruptive business landscape.

You are a great leader, coach, and mentor.
You were born to win, and are predestined for great things!

www.CareerLeadershipCoachingToday.com

Acknowledgments

A master key is a key that will open all the locks in a set, even though each lock has its different key.

I would first like to thank **my mother and father,** who planted the keys, seeds of hope, and inspiration when I was a little girl, telling me I can do anything I want, and to always strive to learn.

To the happy memory of my father. He always called me, my sisters 'Shasha' he explained the meanings as 'the best' in Shona language and 'Mwenewazvo' meaning owner of all things great. May my father rest in peace.

I want to honour and thank **my paternal grandparents and maternal grandfather,** whom although I never met, my parents spoke how they taught them the values of forgiving and loving others as one would like to be treated.

Great honour and thanks to **my maternal grandmother Elizabeth,** who taught me what beauty looked like as she always adorned herself with lovely earrings, and loved dressing up. She was a true heroine. She always talked about Father Cripps and the Church and services at Maronda Mashanu

To **my sister Joyce and my three brothers** for teaching me so much.

To **all the children who call me Mummy D**, I love you. You are my heroes and "sheroes" as leaders of tomorrow.

To **my sister Ethel and Tomas** for their unreserved love and genius, and for encouraging me to stay focused and cope with life's challenges.

To **my sister Jennifer, and Webster, Milosh, Tatiana, Josiah, Joshua, Adana, Eugene, Zara, Jamal, Nevaeh khayal, Zak, Hilary, Lawrence, and Alexander, and my brothers Gerald and Ambs.**

Roger, I love you for encouraging me to create space to do the best and to strive for more, with a focus, and for encouraging me to remain focused. I thank my children, your children, and their spouses for inspiring me in their different ways.

To **Emily and Oliver** for being caring and unassuming.

To my fantastic coach and mentor, **Raymond Aaron,** one of the world's best coaches. Thank you for teaching me so much, and I also thank your team for encouraging me to write this book, and for encouraging me every step of the way. Due to the wisdom and energy of those around me, I was able to get my book done so quickly. Also, thank you to his team, **Liz Ventrella and Tracy Knepple,** for their guidance and expertise on helping me finish this book.

To **Dr. Webb,** for inspiring and being so kind and supportive. Doctors' tongues give hope and encouragement. I appreciate you, everyone in your team, and your family.

To the inspiring individuals on Club House: **Rob Moore@Progressive, Tina D. Lewis, Les Brown, Rob Moore, Manny Fernandes, John Lee, Peter Horna, Ella Matheson, Ayn Assaf, Snoop Dogg, Venessa Tafur, Julian Broadus, Dr. Payel Gupta, Dr. Alpi Patel, Dave Kerpen, and Sara McCord,** to name a few. Thank you.

◎To **MBA alumni group at Kingston University.**

To all MBA lecturers at Kingston University who were so committed to coaching and mentoring me to pass my MBA: **Dr. Sirhey Kovela, Dr. Christina Butler, Dr. Marvyn Boatswain, Dr. Elena Fitkov-Norris, Dr. J. Miguel Imas, Dr. Pauline Parker, Dr. Jelena Petrovic, and Mrs. Deborah Pinder-Young.**

To all the **MBA fellow graduates, Luke, Matt, Marcin, Grace MBA Russian students in my cohort, especially Elena Kuznetosva.** Thank you for being such a caring and motivating human being.

To my **Photography teacher and mentor Mark**, thank you, I appreciate all your help

Olivia Hepburn, Patricia, Maria, Fumi Caitlyn.

Olive Gallimore, thank you for your friendship.

To all **lecturers at Hull University** who coached and mentored me to achieve my master's degree in social work.

To **all lecturers at the University of North London**, now Metropolitan University, for all the support, teaching, and mentoring, and coaching me to pass my BA (Honours) in international business and economics.

To **Phil Treleven,** programme manager at the time who mentored, coached and inspired me to learn more about project management when I worked at Energis Telecoms.

To **Ann Sullivan,** director at Cable and Wireless, global mobile team at the time who mentored me to strive to understand project management, motivated me to aim for the bigger picture, and challenged me to invest in my first property.

To consultant Miss **Sarah E. Clark (SEC) and team,** you are amazingly caring, sensitive, and encouraging, with much love and respect.

To all at Success Resources, Wealth Masters, pouring out nuggets of knowledge, in the UK and South Africa: **Robert and Kim Kiyosaki; Veronica Chan and Richard Chan; Lisa Nichols; Mirela Sula; Paul O'Mahony, San Francisco; Suzie Carder; Robin Banks; Sandy Jadeya; Olind Chapel (future nurse); and Les Brown.**

To **Simon**, my accountant, for always helping me submit my tax to the inland revenue on time.

To all the children, parents, adults, youths, teachers, nurses, doctors, and other clients I met while working to safeguard vulnerable children and adults.

To all the social workers and the peer managers that I worked with throughout the years. They have given feedback on the complex work I was involved in, and have benefitted from my coaching, mentoring, training, and motivation, focusing on their strengths and what they do best. It gave me the confidence that a strength-focused model approach reaps benefits. I have always endeavoured to focus on peoples' strengths, with a client-centred and solution-based approach. I have read more than 100 books on leadership, coaching, psychotherapy, and motivation. **Carl Rogers** developed a non-directive technique. This process allows the client to gain a clearer understanding of their inner thoughts. I have supported clients to find their solutions for the best outcomes.

To **Elaine Hilides,** for your encouragement and for shedding light on 3P principles.

Trevor and family for always being there when I have needed help during the time I ran my recruitment company and your help in the office, help with the website and practical support. Thank you.

To **Staff and management at Recruitment and Employment Confederation** for all the training and support.

To **staff and management at Bullhorn** for the CRM support you offered.

A lot of lessons, I have gained over the years through listening to radio and podcasts. I want to thank the following radio stations that have inspired me through the years:

Dorset Podcast
Hope FM
Classical Music FM
Abbey 104
Air 107.2
BBC Dorset FM
BBC Radio Solent
The Breeze (North Dorset)
Fire Radio
Greatest Hits Radio South Coast
Heart Dorset New Forest
Heart Solent
Heart South
Hot Radio
Nerve Radio
Original 106 Solent
Vale FM and Wave 105
Wessex FM

During the lockdown, I listened to these stations and learned a lot while driving around Dorset, working, and doing my grocery shopping.

To the most amazing people in the whole world, I am incredibly grateful.

To **Dr. Pauline Parker** for her life-changing teaching and unparalleled ability to help others. I am honoured to be able to call her my supervisor, mentor, and coach.

To **Dr Chapman** for words of encouragement, your kindness, inspiration about well-being and exercising. You and your team are amazingly helpful, making the world a better place through your humanity.

To MBA lecturers **Dr. George Alexandrou and John Fannagan**, whose coaching in financial management helped me realise the need for each individual to understand how money matters, as well as the reading and understanding of multi-national companies. I understand the need for relying on fundamentals of attention to detail, return on investments, and control of costs. This insight peaked my interest in responsible forex trading and investing in stocks and shares to gain financial freedom.

To **Kent Springdal,** Business Educator thank you for your support at KU, I appreciate.

To my lecturer, **Ben Aker,** for your responsible management training, and for inspiring me to challenge my thinking. In every organisation, I should consider their responsible management strategies; salaries for factory workers; fairness of pay; gender gap; fairness to all people, regardless of race, gender, or age; and inclusion policies that accommodate those with disabilities, mental health issues, or any diagnosis. Global leaders, politicians and businesses have a responsibility and accountability that their activities and products do not negatively impact on communities including children, women and men, the environment or climate change. We all have a responsibility to save our planet for current and future generations.

Plant-based food and diet is a hot topic and impacts on each individual's health and well-being.

To **Richard Bandler** for teaching me the insights found in neuro-linguistic programming.

To **Dorset Chamber of Commerce** for all the business ideas you teach and share; thank you. **Ian Girling,** Chief Executive of the Chamber of Commerce, thank you for all your assistance.

To **Chinmai Swamy,** for your help and assistance.

To **Tracy Knepple,** for your assistance and help.

To **Jane Webb and her husband, David**, for being so kind and unassuming and encouraging. I am grateful for insights I received from early morning gym colleagues and the deep-sea swimming tribe, and for them keeping showing up for their individual "keep fit and well-being" regime, and for inspiring me to stick to the consistent habit of early morning exercises.

To **Sue Draper,** thank you for inspiring me. Your unfailing daily early morning habit of walking your lovely dogs, come rain, snow or sunshine. The beautiful, creative and amazing paintings you do. Our walls are decorated with your inspiring art work and we celebrate you as your paintwork brings such calmness and joy. You are so gifted and kind, raising funds for the Forest Holme charity. May God continue to bless you and your family. I learned so much from your inclusiveness, thoughtfulness and kindness. You make the world a better place at such a time as this.

To **Mary Wilson and her husband, David,** who are very kind people, thank you.

To **Paul Stephenson, wife, and the boys,** for your inspiration and motivation, and for sharing the passion of your businesses, longevity, transformation. Three day working week sounds great. You helped me to view business situations differently and thank you for sharing books to read.

To **Carolie, Gerom and Samuel,** thank you for being so king.

Rick Stein management and staff, thank you for being so king, such a lovely space to sit for tea and meals, to reflect and to write.

To **Colin**, personal trainer, the team at Water Sports Academy for supporting my 13-year-old nephew Josiah at the time for inspiring the importance of keeping fit from a young age to develop discipline.

To **Theresa and Jerry,** with your early morning daily walking, you show up and have often waited to see if I am safe when I sea swim. You encourage and motivate me. Thank you.

To **Marianne Peckham, husband Roger, and family,** for the love, inspiration, sharing of prayers, and gratitude to the church community.

To **Jean Chambers, Mary, and the Viva Voice Choir,** as they are such amazing singers and continued work raising funds for charities. I have always enjoyed Wednesday night music and singing practice and the few theatre performances I was involved in. Thank you for the opportunity.

My grandmother used to tease me when I told them I was going to play, and I would always be found at the local church, **Reverend Dr Guti and wife** at Forward In Faith which was across the road near our family home where I learned how to play the piano and guitar. I am grateful. This was a safe space for my sisters, brothers, and me when we were little.

To **Bishop Nick,** who confirmed at the Salisbury Cathedral.

To **Reverend Andrew O'Brien and his wife; Reverend Thomas Pelham and his wife; and everyone from church** for your prayers.

To **Father Simon Clarke,** whose support and prayers for my mother and my family has been so great; he is so kind and generous.

To **Michele Graby** for being an inspiration, and to **Munya, Rochford, Sharon, Lettie, Melannie, Delroy, Iyabo, Tapuwa,** for your support during the time I worked with you in Bucks. **Marco, Alex, Isaac in Sutton.**

To **Frances Elue** for the joint course content formation and delivery, of coping with working virtually and the stress, well-being, and wellness team development sessions during the COVID-19 lockdown. To **Sharon, Munya, Rochford, Melanie, Lettie.**

To **Maria Dennis** for all the encouraging and morning daily uplifting messages for prayers and medication.

To **Paul Butler** for having confidence in me and giving me my first care management, hospital social work and auditing job, with the responsibility to ensure safe discharge plans were in place, in close liaison with doctors and nurses.

In memory of the late **Father Arthur Cripps:** My mother speaks of how he inspired her and my maternal grand-parents through prayers, and his kindness also inspired my mother so much. To this day, she speaks highly of him for having a profoundly positive impact on her and her family; and in turn, she has been able to instil gratitude, prayer, forgiveness, and medication values in me.

To **Vik Mistry** and team for the support and the opportunities to work on projects, to coach, and to offer training, mentoring and motivation to new recruits in the recruitment and consulting space. I appreciate.

To **Stella Kikoyo,** thank you for being inclusive and encouraging the identifying of gifts in those you lead.

To **Sandra Olita, Sally, Tia, Catherine, Ola, Faith, Ratha, Panashe, Yasinta, Sebastian, Evelyn,** thank you.

To **Ali Matthews,** thank you for giving everyone a fair chance and not tolerating bullying in the workplace.

To **Kendra Bell** for being such a woman of inspiration, and a leader.

To **Sharon Taylor,** thank you for always being encouraging.

To **Tim Nelson** for inspiring me to strive for more; thank you.

To **Angie** in Birmingham, for being so helpful. You are genuinely kind and giving. Thank you.

To **Mama Addoyobo Essuman and husband, Fifi;** thank you for being such good friends, and for your support. You always cheer me on to do the greater good.

To **Helen Downs and her husband, Mark,** for their support and encouragement.

To **all of my friends** for being such amazing people and for inspiring me every day. They encourage me to take risks, learn new things, and be the best person that I can be. My friends are truly remarkable people, and I am so lucky to have each and every one of them in my life.

To **my cousins** for teaching me to look at life through a different lens.

To **Dr. Wahid Eskander** for his encouragement and support.

To **Tim Matthews, his wife, and church members,** Swithun's-Strocks and St. Clément's, thank you for motivating the community.

To **Jo Keegan, Jack and team.** I am grateful for all your help.

Semone Fraser, you are a true Lioness and CEO. Thank you for the words of encouragement and support.

To **Liz Lean Public Relations** for taking time to read my enquiry. Thank you.

To **Simone Fraser,** for being a lioness and inspiration. Thank you.

To **Paul and Royston** for being helpful and considerate neighbours.

To **all Coolhurst neighbours,** thank you for being good neighbours.

To the team at **Taylor Made Estate** agent, your Luxury and Prestige monthly magazine with beautiful homes is always inspiring.

To **Ann**, my deep-sea swimming partner, you encourage and inspire me. All the work you do to repair sailing dinghy moth, I always look forward to catching up with you.

To **the team at Dorset Living,** your monthly magazine is always informative.

To **the team at Anglotown,** for your support, thank you.

To all **managers and staff at FJB hotels,** you are all amazing, thank for making life so enjoyable always smiling, kind and helpful thank you.

To **Daniele Lechon,** future nurse, you can do it, her manager and team, thank you.

Dr A Chakrabarti for your kind help and support. One of my clients once said to me doctors and nurses give life with the words they use. You make a difference to the world.

To **Hannah and everyone on the team,** this is true. Thank you.

To **Grace and Sara Rawlings,** your genuine inclusiveness and love for everyone is always evident. Thank you for making the world a better place. You are a ray of sunshine.

To **Don**, you inspire! Running every morning is a habit you maintain come rain or thunder, and is an inspiration to the sea swimming group. Thank you.

To the late **Dr Myles Munroe and Nelson Mandela,** whose teachings continue to inspire and are so relevant in today's world.

To **T.D Jakes, Michael Jordan, Erik Schmidt, Jonathan Rosenberg, Joyce Meyer, Brian Houston, Hill Song, Kim Walker, Kari Jobe, Steve Harvey, Stephen Furtick, Nick Vujicic,** thank you for the motivating, inspirational and life-changing content you share.

To **Sir Alex Ferguson,** thank you for being such legend; kind, unassuming and such an inspiration. You, your wife and friends allowed my sister, her baby and me to get your spot when we were all waiting for a taxi in Monaco. Such humility. You are a true leader everywhere you go. In front of the camera or not.

To **Sir Harry Rednapp,** thank you for being so unassuming. You show humanity, and you are inclusive and share nuggets of knowledge. When asked for photos, you also kindly allowed me to take not one, not two, but three. I appreciate. You made my day.

Thank you to **Prince Harry and Meghan** for the work on Mental Health Awareness, and the work you do to advocate for women and the disadvantaged.

Thank you to **Oprah Winfrey**, and **Michelle and Barack Obama** for the positive work you continue to do to support the disadvantaged, and give a voice to women.

Thank you to **Forbes Riley and team** for all the amazing transformational and life changing teachings you are doing as mentors, coaches and teachers.

Foreword

Do you feel stuck, either personally or professionally? *The Book on Career Leadership Coaching Today: Empowering Leaders to Maximize Strengths and Talents to Excel!* gives you the 10 Master Keys to unlocking your potential through coaching and mentoring. Lady Doris Choto is based in the UK she takes her years of project work experience for multi-national companies, local government, mentor, trainer and coach, distilling them into tips and tools that you can use right now to inspire major change in your life.

With each key, Doris taps into potential obstacles, and shows you how to use your inner leader to find creative and innovative solutions. No matter what issue your business is facing, *The Book on Career Leadership Coaching* can provide a viable way to find the solution within your team or yourself. Doris focuses on building up strengths and avoiding the trap of focusing solely on addressing weaknesses. With her skilled direction, you can find and release your inner leader and tap into that success, and help others do the same.

If you are looking for a guide to take your leadership to the next level, *The Book on Career Leadership Coaching Today: Empowering Leaders to Maximize Strengths and Talents to Excel!* is the resource you need!

Raymond Aaron
New York Times Bestselling Author

Prologue

The word "career," for both men and women, means an occupation undertaken for a significant period of a person's life, with opportunities for progress.

To every woman and man leader, the world has changed dramatically, and the saying "job for life" is a thing of the past. Since the COVID-19 lockdown in 2020, everyone has stories to tell about the disruptions to businesses as we adapted to working from home. That transition brought its own challenges, including increased screen time, isolation, those parents and caregivers having children under the same roof 24/7 as they could not attend school, older people in care homes isolated, for those parents caring for children with disabilities facing challenges without any assistance. All the demands of home working were balanced against running businesses virtually, or the waves of work that seemed never-ending. The divide between work and home was like a dam that had given way, and many families struggled with this new reality. This indeed is the **Fourth Industrial Revolution** as we also experience the confusion of boundaries between the physical, digital, and biological worlds. The mixture of advances in artificial intelligence (AI), robotics, the Internet of Things (IoT), 3D printing, genetic engineering, quantum computing, and other technologies is now imbedded in our day to day lives.

No doubt, the impact has caused different levels of stress. Only time will tell. All of us grapple with unanswered questions as we navigate the new world order and its impact on us personally and professionally.

Companies like Amazon, Apple, Tesla, Microsoft, Google, and Facebook, Zoom to mention a few, have thrived, given the nature of their internet-based business model. Artificial intelligence, big data, and infographics are the foundations of a decentralised revolution. Our reality is full of different apps, from TikTok to LinkedIn. Within this mass of media, we still are looking for meaningful connections in a world turned upside down by the pandemic.

Other companies benefiting are Nio (NIO) Nio dominates Chinese **electric vehicle** innovation with its line of vehicles, charging stations and more.

Xpeng (XPEV) ...
Fisker (FSR) ...
Tesla (TSLA) ...
Tesla's Impact and Current Performance. ...
Chargepoint (CHPT) ...
Blink Charging (BLNK)

Disruptive new technologies include BEV's (battery electric vehicle) which are 100% electric, and PHEV's (Plug-in electric hybrid vehicles) which have a battery and an electric motor, but also have an internal combustion engine. PHEVs drive on electric sometimes, and gasoline or diesel once the battery is depleted.

During Covid-19 Lockdown, Government guidance encouraged working from home, while key worker parents faced the dilemma of sending their to school including children classified as vulnerable where safe-guarding concerns were identified. For everyone else, they were required to stay at home, with the only exception being going out for food shopping, hospital appointments, or exercising. In the absence of face-to-face working conditions in most industries, meetings are held via video conference apps, such as Zoom, Teams, and Skype.

While the technology has been available for years, the pandemic accelerated its use. Who could have imagined 10 years ago that the commute to your job could be as short as walking into your living room from your bedroom?

Conference platforms have become the order of the day. Have you thrived under these challenging times? Are you an adapter, a leader, and a coach? Staying ahead of the game is the master key to winning, regardless of the challenges that come your way.

Let's dive into the master keys and how you can employ them to amplify your professional success!

Master Key 1

Know Yourself – Who Are You and Why Are You Here?

You might have read that title and be wondering what that has to do with career leadership coaching today. The fact is that life can flow past without you being consciously aware of its passage. Over the years, I have met more than one individual who has told me they woke up and realised they had turned:

Twenty – They wondered how time had already flown and they were on their own.

Thirty – Their career was not where they imagined it would be, but they had no idea how to accelerate the process.

Forty – That career slump of their thirties has become a giant rut, filled with frustration and stress.

Fifty – There was the shock of realising the life changes they would have wanted, along with their dreams and goals going unfulfilled.

Sixty – At this point, it dawned on them that all these years of working had put them no closer to their desired goal. Their passion was elusive as they struggled to understand who they were and what they really wanted to do. It is never too late, no matter what stage of life you are at.

For some they were able to realise their strengths and talents early in life and they have excelled requiring coaching to reach higher levels of themselves.

Yet what if I told you that you did not need to spend a lifetime on the hunt for your passion? Could it be that within each one of us is a leader? You need to understand that each of us is a leader in our different ways. By accepting that you can be coachable, be led, can lead, and also be part of a team, you can transform your business, career, personal relationships, and the world!

As the leader and coach in your life, your business, your work, and your home, you need clear, decisive, strong, assertive, competent, nurturing, emotional, and effective communication, regardless of whether you are a man or a woman. Societal prejudices may try to interfere, but I encourage you to be a voice and advocate if you notice colleagues using words that reinforce negative bias and stereotypes. Understanding yourself is one of the master keys to your development and growth in today's changing world. Throughout this book, I guide you to the master keys of leadership through coaching. You can take this knowledge and pass it down as a legacy to the next generation.

As a leader in the home, as either a parent or caregiver, you are responsible for teaching children critical skills and tools from an early age. By inculcating them before your children are 13, you give them a solid foundation to be a leader in their own lives.

Before you can lead, it is essential to understand who you are and who you want to become. With this exercise, I want you to find a quiet space where you can reflect and be still. Give yourself this gift of quiet, which is incredibly vital in this busy world we all inhabit. Take a journal or notebook with you, so that you can jot down your thoughts during this period of reflection.

Throughout this exercise, be truthful with yourself. Do not make excuses. Just concentrate on who you are and who you want to become. Is that unclear? Then start with figuring out what you are good at and what you naturally gravitate towards. What is your passion? What activities make you lose track of time because you are so passionate about them and become completely immersed? Once you have jotted down a few of these things, it is time to move on to relationships.

As you take stock of your relationships, I want you to think about who you are in that space. Do the relationships bring out the best in you, or do they tend to be negative, bringing out the worst in you?

For you to lead and coach others, you must know yourself. My father used to like Karate and Bruce Lee, the Kung Fu legend who said, "Research your own experience. Absorb what is useful, reject what is useless, and add what is specifically your own." Here are a few questions to consider during this time of research and reflection into your experiences and personal journey to date.

- Who am I in this changing world?
- What is my purpose?
- What was I born to do?
- What is my plan for the next 6 months, the next year, the next 2, 3, 5, and 10 years?
- Why does my family not appreciate all that I do?
- Why do I feel less confident about what I am good at anymore?
- Why do I feel overwhelmed and afraid?
- Why do I lack confidence and feel like an imposter?
- Do I have a strong desire to improve and be innovative?
- I am running a successful business or career, so how come I am not happy?
- I have limited financial resources and am struggling. Why am I not happy?
- Do I have extra streams of income?
- Do I have a life insurance policy?
- People I went to school with are achieving greater levels of success. Where did I go wrong?
- How can I motivate those around me to work and be accountable?
- Everything is changing in my business and industry. How can the workers and I deliver what is required to meet the needs of the customers?
- Why do I feel that I have to do everything myself so that nothing goes wrong?
- Why are the people I lead not inspired and driven, particularly during this challenging and disruptive COVID-19 lockdown?
- Are my daily habits leading me to the next level, or hindering my success?

Each of these questions might appear simple on the surface, but they are geared to helping you think about what is possible and where you might be creating obstacles for yourself in terms of your leadership. Let's start our journey by looking at your daily habits and how they might be holding you back.

Daily Habits

Habit(s) is defined as a settled or regular tendency or practice, especially one that is hard to give up. They form many of the aspects of your daily routine. Think about the first parts of your day. You get up, brush your teeth, change your clothes, brush your hair, grab your breakfast, and—before the COVID-19 lockdown—head out the door. With working from home, what daily habits do you follow? Most of those things you do automatically, without any conscious thought at all. Those automatic responses and habits have brought you to this place. When I work with a client, they tend to be struggling with:

- Job dissatisfaction
- Weight issues
- A lack of consistency
- A tendency to give up quickly
- A lack of focus
- Attracting and maintaining relationships with people who bring negative energy or bring out the worst in others

- Being unhappy with the amount of money they have in the bank
- Lacking the skills to make money work for them, like the 1% of the population

Can you identify with any of those thoughts or feelings? Recognise that the habits you formed have played a large role in shaping your current reality. Not every habit is a bad one, but those unhealthy ones contribute to your inability to attain your desired goals. Habits have shaped your life. They may keep you from experiencing your best life. Your habits could lead to a way of thinking that devalues you through unhealthy decisions. If that is the case, then I am giving notice to your unhealthy habits and the negative thinking they foster. IT IS TIME FOR A CHANGE!

The challenge is that you cannot simply just try to eliminate bad habits. That leaves a void where other unhealthy or bad habits can creep back in. Instead, for every bad habit you want to eliminate, replace it with an equivalent healthy habit. Think about your daily routine. Does it include time for you to pray, meditate, eat healthy, and have time to be active or exercise? Perhaps you can identify timewasters or habits that have blocked you from including these healthy habits. Start by planning out your daily routine and what you want to include. What do you include in your relaxation time, be it special activities or hobbies that bring you joy? Do you give yourself time to think, or spend all day rushing frantically around, making your mind feel like it is spinning constantly? When you do not have time for your mind to be quiet and calm, to relax from the daily grind, then your sleep patterns can be negatively impacted.

One of my mentors taught me to stick to habits that contribute to my success. You are a leader, which means you are the head, not the tail. Before you can embrace your inner leader, you need to implement habits that are supportive. Coaching can be a critical way to seek the wisdom, honesty, and collaboration necessary to identify those that do not contribute to your success.

Some habits can also contribute to your stress, especially those that contribute to a lack of organisation. With your unwavering desire to succeed, you need to identify habits that are contributing to disorganisation and poor time/task/ financial management.

I love deep-sea swimming and commit to doing this every morning with other deep-sea swimmers, throughout the year as part of my daily habits. Of course, there have been exceptions for being out of the country, or if an emergency disrupts this routine. Then I have the backup of taking a walk or cycling. The goal is that even if it looks different from day to day, I am getting some form of physical exercise. The COVID-19 lockdown presented a challenge with social distancing guidelines, but I found that if I stagger when I go swimming, those guidelines could be followed.

Part of building good and healthy habits is being diligent during the early days. After all, when you are creating a new habit, it requires you to be conscious of completing that habit daily. The automatic and subconscious aspect is not yet fully engaged. My grandmother told me about ants. These ants tackled massive projects with consistency and diligence.

Habits of indolence and indulgence grow upon people. It is easy to give up on a good habit if you are not diligent and allow other things to get in the way. Therefore, life can run to waste and poverty. It might appear to be at a distance, but gradually, from not being diligent and determined to form new habits, it draws near, as the saying goes. Your thoughts towards wealth and financial independence are important, and the habits you use to move you towards that independence are vital. You are important and your voice matters.

Now let's talk about another challenge that could limit your leadership abilities, which is fear.

Fear

Every one of us has dealt with fear at some point in our lives. That fear could be of failure, of disappointing others, or even the fear of disappointing ourselves. Our minds can build up a situation to the point that fear ends up paralysing us from making any decisions at all. For some people, facing relationship breakdowns, a health challenge, or a course exam can cause them to be afraid.

Fear can fuel procrastination, which is a time thief, stealing opportunities and our focus. Many people I have met throughout my personal and professional relationships have expressed some type of fear. As we dig down into their fear, it becomes apparent that their fear is holding them back from achieving their purpose and realising their dreams.

Here are a few examples of fear as it could present itself in your life:

- Fear of making decisions that change your life
- Fear of the unknown
- Fear of starting your own business
- Fear of learning a new skill
- Fear of moving to a new area
- Fear of imposter syndrome
- Fear of missing out (FOMO)
- Fear of applying for a job
- Fear of asking for a promotion
- Fear of resigning, even when you know the job is not right for you, because you fear never finding another position
- Fear of starting over again when things have not gone the way you anticipated in any area of your life
- Fear of commitment
- Fear of travelling and exploring new things

Think about the individuals you know. They might have lived in an area for years, even decades. Yet despite all that time in one place, they do not know the area well enough to recommend places for you to visit. Their fears of the unknown have kept them from making the decision to get to know their hometown. Thus, they miss out on the pleasures of local leisure activities and getting to know the unique history of their hometown.

The reason I focus on this example is because it can be a small thing, but fear and a routine can keep you locked into a path that is no longer healthy for you. Throughout the coaching process, my goal is to help you understand the ways that your fears could be undermining you as a leader, both personally and professionally.

Your decisions, backed by action and clarity of purpose, are the foundation of success. Without knowing what you do not want in your life, you cannot identify what you do want. Even when you are asked what you want, it is natural to first list all the things you don't want. Instead of fighting that natural tendency, just go with it, and clear the negative so that you can focus on how you want your life to look.

As part of clearing the negative, make a list of what is going on right now that fuels negative feelings and energy. List your feelings regarding events and situations that might be fuelling your fears or anxiety. Once you know what is driving those feelings, then you can determine the best plan to address those issues.

Facing your fear of the unknown in disruptive situations is one of life's constants, something to tackle head on. Anything that is worth doing is worth doing badly until you get it right. Allow yourself to appreciate the journey of failing. It will bring incredible wisdom your way.

When I was a child, we used to recite this mantra in Sunday school: "Try, try, try again. If at first you do not succeed, try again." Many spiritual books talk about the dangers in the world that seek to destroy our spirit and inner leadership. We have to be on guard so that our dreams and goals are not stolen from us. By utilising coaching and mentorship, we can keep an eye on our time. Thus, it will not slip away. Time is the most valuable currency that you possess. Once the time is gone, you cannot earn or buy it back. Procrastination steals our time and motivation. Why put off till tomorrow what you could accomplish today?

Our bodies have an internal rhythm, tied to the universe. Listen to it, and allow that internal clock to awaken you, focused and ready to tackle the day. That energy that you project by acknowledging your ties to the universe, will impact those around you. Still, even with your example, others might not follow. The road to life is straight and narrow. To follow it, you need to be willing to do the things that others will not do.

Discipline Is Important in Every Area of One's Life

Building good habits or effectively leading yourself and others starts with a level of discipline. The undisciplined life is filled with failure. This type of failure does not lead to wisdom but to excuses and wasted time. Believe in yourself, and act on your dreams by disciplining yourself to have actions and habits that will move you closer to achieving those dreams and goals. Here are some ways that you can bring a greater level of discipline into your daily routine.

- Write down little tasks in the morning to clear your head.
- Start the day with exercising to keep fit.
- Ask yourself if things will matter in a day, week, month, or year, prioritising tasks.
- Make it a point to look at different industries to continue to develop your own unique business concepts.

- See the potential in others, and acknowledge strengths in others. When people help you and give you ideas, acknowledge them and give them credit. This is a great leadership trait.
- As people are bombarded with multiple emails, only check your communications at specific times in your day, if your job does not involve safeguarding issues. Doing so will help you to avoid being distracted from your priorities.

The world has a pattern of undisciplined thoughts that lead to undisciplined actions. The Bible encourages us to not conform our minds to this way of thinking, but to "be transformed by the renewing of your mind." One of the best ways to renew our minds is to be conscious of what we are feeding our minds. The type of entertainment, books, and even friends we associate with, all play a part in shaping our thoughts and actions. When I am disciplined enough to choose differently in these areas, I see the difference in my mind, which is renewed.

In business, it can be easy to get overwhelmed by all the different aspects that come up. I personally experienced this as I tried to successfully run businesses in the past, only to become overwhelmed and end up losing thousands of pounds that I had invested. These experiences led me to commit to not be a person who promises what they cannot deliver. Instead, I picked myself up and went to university to study for my master's in social work. This educational experience was a chance for me to start again.

However, I also continued my work as a property investor. Our inner leader can guide us to explore multiple options and diversify in our personal and professional lives. I found that as a property investor, I learned many different lessons. Failure gave me wisdom. For instance, I found that tenants would go months without paying any rent. I opted to use established estate agents to manage my properties, allowing their expertise to help me avoid those types of tenants. This example is just one of many, but it shows how being disciplined and open to learning can be key to absorbing lessons and acting upon them.

As a property investor, I needed discipline and organisation. I have managed my property portfolio with the help of a team of different estate agents, carpenters, electricians, plumbers, builders and my accountant, for over the past 20 years, to keep on top of things. Even then, various estate agents have let me down. Despite paying my management fees to manage the property and collect rents, these agents have let tenants not pay rent for months. Staying calm in these situations is a challenge, as tenants can claim harassment. Always remember to act professionally, stay calm, and be reasonable. Set the tone for your estate agents and your team as you lead them when facing these circumstances.

As I mentioned, your actions could be used by the tenant to claim harassment. Depending on your country's laws or local regulations, you may not enter the property without permission, remove their belongings, or change the locks. To evict a non-paying tenant, you need to follow the proper legal procedures through the courts. It will protect you as the landlord. I love to teach others how to navigate these situations, and more, for those interested in property investment. As a leader, you must give direction and take advantage of teachable moments to increase the knowledge and wisdom of all your team members.

My father used to say, "Once beaten, twice shy." The challenges I have faced as a single mum—studying full time for my first degree, in international business and economics; my second degree, a master's in social work; and then later, part time for my MBA; and working full time—required me to apply discipline. I had to apply for mitigating circumstances (a challenging process on its own). Then, as I got into a new work routine after graduation, my life was upended by a breast cancer scare. A couple of operations and a change in your health can profoundly affect your whole world. In my full-time job, I was allowed three months of full-time pay as part of my health leave. Then it was reduced in the fourth month. Can you imagine what would have happened if I did not have any other income streams? This made me realise that I need to help other people to plan for financial freedom and not depend on a job's salary. With God's help, I had to master my thought process to avoid falling into fear or despair. If you need counselling in any area of your life, seek it out. Part of being disciplined means seeking out help or guidance when facing challenging circumstances.

I am always learning new things. I love learning. Discipline helps me to make time for reading and opportunities to grow my knowledge base. Research shows that the average number of books read by leaders, such as CEOs, is 60 books annually. That is five books a month. Oprah Winfrey once said, "What I know for sure is that reading opens you up. It exposes you and gives you access to anything your mind can hold."

I have always been curious about the human mind, emotions, communication and how people deal with and cope with trauma. I attended level 1 and 2 counselling courses in 2005, which prompted me to pursue NLP. I also attended psychotherapy training part time for four years, to learn more about myself and also gain a better understanding of how people cope under stress, and what can lead to self-defeating behaviours. This course helped me to really understand psychodynamics, human behaviour, lack of confidence, self-defeating behaviours, depression, hypnosis, dealing with anxiety, and the mindset of people that are trying to lose weight, stop smoking, or are dealing with fear and stress. As a coach, I am equipped to help clients and others deal with these issues.

Leading and coaching people presents its own challenges. With the increasing number of people working from home due to the COVID-19 lockdown, personal challenges that might not be apparent are bubbling just below the surface. Some people have adjusted to this type of working arrangement, but some continue to struggle.

As leaders and coaches, we need to be mindful that some people have children with disabilities, some have their own disabilities, and some live-in home environments with other psychological pressures, and may be dealing with more limited space than before. Going to work presented an opportunity to escape from their personal home challenges, and it was a means of obtaining some form of respite. For some, working at home presents other challenges as they are not able to work in a quiet and office-like environment.

Leadership is the art of motivating a group of people to act towards achieving a common goal. In a business setting, this can mean directing workers and colleagues with a strategy to meet the company's needs.

Leadership for both men and women is a process of social influence, which maximizes the efforts of others, towards the achievement of a goal. Notice key elements of this definition. Leadership itself stems from social influence, not authority or power.

The noun "today" means the present time or age. "The world of today" includes the present moment, as opposed to yesterday or tomorrow. This book is for every leader, man, or woman. Leading in life is more complex, and most people I talk to say that it is more stressful, with the demands of working remotely in the artificial intelligence information/ internet-based space having its own overwhelming outcomes. We cannot pick up on the body language that you would otherwise be able to, during face-to-face interactions. The adaption to holding team meetings, supervision, and most interactions via these video conferencing platforms, also involves the challenges of maintaining security.

Discipline in our habits and thoughts is more necessary than ever before, yet it can also be even more challenging as you face the realities of a pandemic or other major challenging life events.

Gone are the days where people looked at themselves with an employee mentality. Now we recognise more than ever that we are in charge of our mindset, and changes to that mindset require you to be a change maker as a leader, coach, and coachee. Even while you are leading others, you will also be in a position to be led and be coachable. One of my mentors always says that a coachable person becomes a good leader. Sir Alex Ferguson, from the world of professional football, and Paul McGinley, Europe's captain for the Ryder Cup at Gleneagles, Michael Jordan's (MJ) story is one of inspiration. He loved sports but failed to make his high school basketball team as a sophomore. He was disciplined and continued to practice and made the team the next year. After high school he accepted a basketball scholarship to the University of North Carolina, where he played under head coach Dean Smith etc. Today he is worth US1.6 billion. His mindset is that of a competitor: Some of his notable and inspirational quotes we can learn from include:

- "I can accept failure; everyone fails at something. But I cannot accept not trying."
- "I have always believed that if you put in the work, the results will come."
- "I have missed more than 9,000 shots in my career. I have lost almost 300 games. 26 times, I have been trusted to take the game winning shot and missed. I have failed over

and over and over again in my life. And that is why I succeed."

- "My attitude is that if you push me towards something that you think is a weakness, then I will turn that perceived weakness into a strength."
- "If you're trying to achieve, there will be roadblocks. I have had them; everybody has had them. But obstacles do not have to stop you. If you run into a wall, do not turn around and give up. Figure out how to climb it, go through it, or work around it."`(MJ)

One of my coaches told me, if you want to get fit, no one can exercise or go to the gym for you. You have got to discipline ourself, work hard, stretch yourself past your current limits, lapses and failure happen. Reaching and staying at the top requires self-competition, continued self-development, identifying and surrounding yourself with people who challenge you, coach and mentor you to become the best version of your brilliant self.

These are just a few examples. A disciplined and coachable mind sees opportunities to learn instead of being defensive or argumentative. Why do I say this? Wisdom is key. People I speak to always say they want to grow themselves to achieve financial freedom and a better lifestyle. While we all can say the words, the right mindset and actions will help you turn those words into your reality.

With all the disruption to traditional career paths, and the ever-changing landscape of the global market, it presents the questions: "What does career leadership coaching need today? How can it be made relevant in today's disruptive global landscape?"

COVID-19 gave businesses the choice to adapt quickly or die. Those who had the right mindset and a willingness to adapt to this rapidly changing and ongoing situation, were the businesses that were still standing and continued to maintain their success throughout the lockdown. Sadly, a lack of flexibility and adaptation has left some businesses closing their doors. Could it also be the result of not having good coaching?

Great changes at a rapid pace require focused actions right now, not procrastination or excuses. People who might not have been flexible or focused in the past are questioning their status quo and themselves, looking for answers to why they are struggling at this point in their lives when others are thriving, even during a pandemic. This new world order, a shift in organisational behaviour, was a major shift in the operating structure and management culture, demanding different, strategic thinking and leadership.

Think about any successful individual in sports, be it a footballer or an Olympic gold medallist. All of these sports-men and women are not successful on their own. They have a coach to help them reach their maximum potential. To unleash your inner leader and your maximum potential, you need a coach as well. What are your struggles? What things do you need help with to solve? To live effectively means tapping into resources that help you build a legacy. History should reflect your mark on the world.

When I am coaching, I put ten master keys for leaders in place, to achieve organisational common goals, with both individuals and teams. According to the International Coach Federation (ICF), coaching is defined as a partnership with clients, in a thought-provoking and creative process that inspires them to maximize their personal and professional potential.

To understand what a coach does, it is important to understand how the word is defined. Coach, as a noun, is one who instructs or trains another. Coaching means to instruct, direct, prompt, or train intensively by instruction or demonstration.

As a coach, I am not here to give you all the answers. Instead, I help you to find the answers within yourself. You are your own solution. As a coach, I prompt clients to address their challenges by asking the right questions and guiding you as you uncover the answer within. I also help my clients address their challenges by assisting them in getting honest about the behaviours that might contribute to their woes. Together, a coach and client can formulate a plan of action to improve areas of the client's life in a way that works best for them. Along the way, I am demonstrating how to listen, how to learn, and how to lead.

As COVID-19 continues to challenge our global community, discussions have increased about how to support leaders, top teams, and organisations in a volatile, uncertain, complex, and ambiguous (VUCA) world. Coaching can provide a life of support, because it goes beyond leadership.

As organisations, as individuals, as families, and as children or students, we all need aspects of coaching.

Research shows that there are various frameworks and models used in coaching for businesses, nationally and globally. One is Sir John Whitmore's devised GROW model, whose acronym stands for goal, reality, options, and way forward/wrap up or what next (Whitmore et al 2006). However, the focus of this model is on the task, not on the individual. Therefore, it does not put the individual at the centre.

That gap exists without addressing the worker's/student's/individual's attributes and their self-awareness before, during, and after the task, which is likely to impact the desired SMART goal. Your individual attributes are key to goals being specific, measurable, attractive, realistic, and time-bound.

- Are you self-aware?
- Do you have a high emotional intelligence?
- What are your strengths?
- How can you, individually and as part of a team, collaborate from a position of strength?

As leaders, we have been coping with the uncertainties of the COVID-19 crisis. This situation has required strength and resilience as never before, to ensure you continue to stay on top of rapid changes happening, nationally and globally, for businesses, families, and individuals. The need for great leadership cannot be over-emphasised.

Coaching offers a structured and tailored framework to enable you, as a leader and coach, to steer your organisation's ship to achieve a return on its capital and creativity. It involves setting and resetting the aims, goals, and objectives, and developing disruptive new ways of working and supporting growth in the artificial intelligence and internet landscape. Knowing yourself, your strengths, and what drives and motivates you is fundamental to this process.

Finding Inspiration Around You

My mother has always been a storyteller. She told me a story of hard-working birds that would build their own nests by collecting nesting materials. It took a long time to complete. Other birds would watch these hard-working birds, waiting for the moment when they would fly away to look for more nest materials. Then those birds would fly in and steal their nesting material to build their own nests. Which bird are you? Do you swoop in and take advantage of others' hard work, or are you working hard to produce and be effective in your life? Take time to reflect on this, and note your answer.

The moral of this story is that there are people in business and organisations who wait on the side-lines, whilst their colleagues work hard to achieve results for their business. Then those sideliners are happy to step in and claim the credit for the positive results, even if they contributed no input or effort to achieve those results. They gained maximum recognition on the backs of their colleagues.

Leading figures within all organisations need to be cognizant of these predatory behaviours within their businesses, and their negative impact on productivity and working relationships.

My early childhood experiences involve my mum and dad being positive and happy, and providing a united and loving home. There were pictures of their wedding hanging on the walls. My father used to surprise my mother with thoughtful gifts. One evening, he brought a lovely evening dress home and told her they were going to a hotel where a band was performing. He also used to buy birthday cakes and nibbles for us. My father enjoyed football and karate. When discussing politics, he frequently talked about Margaret Thatcher, "the Iron Lady," admiring how she appeared strong and unwavering in her policies and direction. On reflection, perhaps my father wanted to give his daughters the same qualities.

As a business owner, my father was a very positive and inspirational man. He owned a panel beating and spray painting business. He took pride in his work and used to say he was the best panel beater and spray painter of that time. He also used to tell me that I was clever and could do anything I wanted in life. I remember that his confidence in his ability to teach me was so high that he said he could teach me better than my teachers. Needless to say, I went to school with a bit of an attitude. This did not go over well with one of my teachers, who ended up giving me a very hard time. On the other hand, my mother always advised me to be humble, saying that humility is a virtue.

While my parents passed on their wisdom, many of my teachers were inspirational and built my confidence as well. One of my teachers used to call me by my surname and would say, "Choto! You are as proud as a peacock!" I was a prefect and became a deputy head. From an early age, I could not stand children bullying other children. I always intervened to defend those who were being bullied. With hindsight, I guess my coaching and mentoring career started then.

Although my early childhood shaped my confidence in myself, there were also stories of dreams not achieved. My father, for instance, told me started his panel beating business because he was not allowed to practice as an architect, due to the political situation at the time. Later, he met my mother, married her, and had a family. Together, they ran businesses and did well financially. I wonder if that ended up going to my father's head. He eventually left the family home, which was devastating for my siblings and I, even though we did not know or understand why he had left.

My mother took on the mantle of being a single parent, encouraging all of us. She became my rock as she coached and mentored me to focus on my education. As a woman, she recognised how important it was for me to be educated and able to stand on my own two feet, thus providing for myself, my future children, and to help my community. I drew strength and inspiration from her. Although my father left, both of my parents were my first coaches and mentors. They were the first leaders I knew, the ones who taught me to strive to be the best, and to strive to achieve what I wanted. Still, with our changing family situation, I learned early in life that situations and things can change drastically overnight. Thus, COVID-19 has affected everyone around the world, personally and professionally. How can we survive change? By being disciplined, having the ability to set boundaries, and recreating daily routines that support our goals, visions, and objectives.

When I worked in the health and social work landscape, I saw first-hand the traumatic issues that affect child development and well-being, emotionally and psychologically, when children were exposed to abuse and neglect. How children develop and what they experience will later impact their adult relationships. They are complex, emotionally and psychologically. Yet many of the same tactics that I used to safeguard the children I worked with, also applied within my role as a senior practitioner with managerial responsibilities, trainer, mentor, coach and a leader. During my social and managerial work, I found standards when coaching people to help them keep their emotional well-being and self-development on track, through supervision and reflective practice. These are the keys, and I encourage people to draw from these standards because they have helped me personally. I also incorporate these tools into my work with the clients that I coach and mentor, including:

- Asking for feedback
- Using supervision to inform practice
- Using research, theories, and frameworks
- Demonstrating good subject knowledge

- Contributing to an open and creative learning culture
- Reflecting on learning
- Recording learning
- Reflecting on value

Keep a record of your progress. It is essential to your self-knowledge, which grows as you identify the areas where you need further development. That level of personal self-development helped me to keep my career/business progression on track, as I held various senior practitioner roles while running my own business.

I also want to be clear that in the workplace, women and men should be treated equally, which can be challenging for both women and men. In one organisation, a male colleague was involved in a number of projects, serving in a "senior management role." I put myself forward for additional projects, and his response was to contact my manager, saying that I did not have enough work and needed to be kept busy. Other managers should have challenged his perception, because our voices are key to changing how women and men are perceived in the workplace.

For women to step into leadership roles, coaches and leaders need to continue to spread their influence in male-dominated organisational cultures. Research suggests that leaders can also influence organisational culture because they model the primary principles undergirding workplace cultures. Inclusion and a non-judgmental approach is needed when looking at strategic femininity, change agents, and shared power.

In today's world, career leadership coaching should be informed by research, which currently has focused on the challenges that stem from different generations in business and the workplace (Tulgan, 2003). This research looks at varying training and developmental needs, different working styles or preferences, and the impact of changing cultural expectations. In particular, researchers suggest that organisational practices should be generationally appropriate to cater to diverse age groups' needs and demands (Egri & Ralston, 2004; McDonald & Hite, 2008).

Leadership coaching, today, considers the subject of women, recognising the challenges that women leaders have faced over the years, while also looking back at previous generations, today's leaders, and millennials' expectations, both now and beyond, as businesses and careers progress. There is a need to change the way businesses grow future leaders who can excel, regardless of whether they are men or women. Coaches and advocates should give voice to any imbalance, or address any unspoken rules that stand in the way of women or minority groups progressing. It is about giving them the skills and tools to level the playing field. Businesses and organisations benefit when they foster an inclusive culture that allows them to tap into everyone's strengths. Inclusion is the way forward.

With that in mind, let's talk about how your natural strengths and talents can be encouraged through coaching and mentoring.

Master Key 2

Lead Using Your Natural Strengths and Talents

2

While many people tend to think that coaching and mentoring are interchangeable terms, the reality is that each one plays a different part in your self-development, both personally and professionally. Google Scholar explains that **coaching** is more performance-driven, designed to improve a professional's on-the-job performance in a task-specific way. **Mentoring** is more development-driven, looking not just at the professional's current job function but also beyond. It takes a more holistic approach to career development.

Most of the coaches I have spoken to during the COVID-19 crisis, and in its aftermath, noted that coaching has great value in enabling individuals to acknowledge and manage their own trauma reactions and triggers. Coaches seek to connect with and further develop the healthy self, which is better placed to mediate survivor behaviour.

As you are a coach and a leader, before you can step out to help others, it is key to figure out who you are. Knowing yourself is fundamentally important as it will help you understand those you lead or work with, or your relationships.

For a long time, I tried to figure out my own strengths and talents. I was not one of those people that were blessed to know the direction they wanted to go in, from an early age. For example, I have a nephew who is talented in dancing and singing. He was performing at the West End in the UK and Monaco at a very early age. He also travelled to China. His first book, *Wow Wow Wow*, was written at age 13. Josiah, Joshua, and Adana are an inspiration, and so are their parents. My son's children are also talented in their own different ways.

Knowing your children's strengths and talents is essential for you as caregivers or parents, allowing you to channel their energies into a path that aligns with their talents at an early age. Dr. Pauline Parker and Dr. Elisa Back of Kingston University, where I attended my MBA, ran a Young Scientists Virtual Event for children aged 4 to 17, from 1st to 4th June 2021. I had the opportunity to send the link to all the schools that I had links for in the social work space. The teachers could encourage parents to have their children participate, and children would receive certificates of participation. Such opportunities help children develop areas of interest early in their lives, especially students who like science, technology, engineering, and maths.

How can this be done with future leaders?

As a certified Gallup Strengths Coach, understanding the Clifton Strengths Finder (CSF) development helped me gain insight into how each of us can uncover our inner leader. Donald O. Clifton was an educational leader, who established the foundation of the strengths philosophy. It began based on the positive psychology movement, which stresses optimal human functioning and factors that contribute to a sense of well-being and the ability to contribute productively to society (Seligman & Csikszentmihalyi, 2000). Instead of studying mental illness, the movement studies mental health. Don Clifton first designed the interviews that later formed the foundation for the CSF, starting with the question, "What would happen if we studied what is right with people?" (Lopez, Hodges, & Harter, 2005, p. 3).

We all need to employ this positive approach by leaders, parents, children, undergraduates, and MBA/EMBA students. Being supported to understand this approach can help us develop self-awareness and know what our strengths and talents are.

"Knowing yourself is the beginning of all wisdom."
– Aristotle

What a man thinks, so he is.

The definition of wisdom is, *"The quality of having experience, knowledge, and good judgement; the quality of being wise."* In order to develop this quality more fully, we must step out of our comfort zone and work on understanding others, instead of judging. The best leaders work to understand themselves and the members on their teams. As they do, these leaders can maximize the strengths of the individuals to benefit the whole team or organisation. 'There is no 'I' in teams but in win' (Michal Jordan).

Perhaps you had challenges in your childhood that make it hard for you to be understanding to others. The fact that you are reading this book, shows you have led yourself, have persevered, and are resilient. I acknowledge your strengths. Start with embracing yourself and loving who you are, with self-compassion, and allowing yourself to be authentic. As you are reading this book, there is no one else like you in the entire world, created as wonderfully as you—beautiful if you are a woman, handsome if you are a man—that is how precious you are. When we have self-compassion, we can more easily give and receive compassion. There is no one else like you in the world, are unique and precious. You are predestined for great things, and your childhood experiences, good or bad cannot limit you unless you allow them.

The leader in you has always existed. You are a result of competition from conception. From when you were a baby, you led as you learned and mastered new skills. Think of the sequences of fine motor skills you developed in your first few years of life. At three months old, you started playing with your fingers. Up to six months, you had the "palmar grasp reflex" where you gripped with your whole hand. At nine months, you started using your index fingers and your thumb. At 12 months old, you were using your thumb and two fingers to pick up different objects. At 15 months, you were holding a crayon and using it to express your creativity. At 18 months, you had a tripod grip. By the time you were two years old, one hand had become your dominant one. At 2 1/2 years old, you improved your ability to focus on faces, and were confidently walking. You were learning to run, but it did not mean that you did not fall. Even from crawling to walking to running, there were moments when you fell, but you didn't give up. You led yourself towards greater independence from your parents, a process that continued throughout the rest of your childhood and teenage years.

I am just saying this so that you recognise that the leader in you started showing up when you were little. As someone who has coached people dealing with childhood trauma, I could not deny that these traumatic things happened. At the same time, something else is being born. It is a spirit of resilience and strength, and the ability to cope with challenges. When difficult situations happen for these individuals as adults, they tap into that strength, resilience, and coping skills to not only survive but to thrive. The leader in you fights to survive and grow. For example, life's challenges can include a diagnosis, you did not apply for it, it happens, for example, mental health, epilepsy, diabetes, some people can get into circumstances through no fault of their own, for example a partner, husband or wife being promiscuous can result by contracting sexually transmitted diseases which can also be transmitted through blood or drug use through sharing needles or rape. Some people experience a diagnosis of cancer. Research shows that one in eight women will develop breast cancer at some point in their life. This statistic as reported affects all women equally (nationalbreastcancer.org) Breast cancer can be diagnosed through multiple tests, including a mammogram, ultrasound, MRI, and biopsy.

Joan Lunden is an accomplished author, journalist, and television host, and a mother of seven. Her story shows strength, resilience, and overcoming fear. She has a blog, a book titled *Had I Known*, and a live streaming video channel about surviving breast cancer. It has been a helpful resource for me as a woman which can be crucial for women facing early detection. I consider myself favoured, and also fortunate that I found this in the early stages and received help from the breast clinic team and community.

As you go through life, embracing your inner leader involves being strategic and recognising that individuals have gone through different childhood and adulthood experiences. These can include loss, and whether it is losing your job, receiving a diagnosis of an illness (it could be any one of the A to Z listed NHS diseases), losing an opportunity, or having the loss of a relationship, loss is an inevitable part of life. These experiences can also include failure and setbacks.

Establish your moral compass, master your mind, and overcome the story you tell yourself of not being good enough (impostor syndrome). Be encouraged; whatever diagnosis you have, it does not define you, and you are not alone. Everyone suffers from some form of health problem, which may require medication, or blood tests every six months. Whether it is mental health, diabetes, asthma, MS, epilepsy, depression, cancer, or HIV etc, the fact that you receive a specialist's medical input, and know how to manage these health problems, you should be encouraged. Scientific research and development is ongoing in all these medical areas, to come up with solutions to heal and eradicate world poverty and ill health. No one applies to be sick or have a disease, but it can happen to anyone. Strive to have a balanced lifestyle, and invest in yourself no matter what. Gift yourself, nourish yourself with healthy eating, and exercise. Be disciplined about how you take care of yourself. In the 24 hours that each person experiences, gift yourself with one hour of meditation, prayer, and exercise. Just one hour! You deserve it.

As a leader, naturing innovation, enterprise and creativity your understanding that you lead teams with individuals that may be experiencing different life challenges, you need to recognise that those experiences can bring depth to your team. Therefore, your key role is to make sure that everyone is heard, while setting the tone for your team by not being judgmental regarding anyone's experiences and identity. Innovation, enterprise and creativity stems from difference and healthy competition. Healthy competition means you want to succeed but also derive joy from seeing others succeed. Your competitive spirit comes from a growth mindset (Mindset of Excellence: Think and Grow Rich and Believe in Yourself) and is used in a positive way to help your team and yourself reach individual and team goals.

You are a product of competition. Research shows that it takes only one sperm cell to fertilise a woman's egg, but there is stiff competition for that honour. In fact, the average ejaculation contains 200 million sperm. Wow! As you read this book, recognise that you have already won the competition to become a human on this planet we call Earth.

Various impediments exist that sperm must overcome as they travel through the female reproductive tract, including the acidic pH of the vagina, the mucus microarchitecture of the cervix, the narrow uterotubal junction, and the presence of phagocytosing leukocytes in the vagina, cervix, and uterus. Amazingly, all of us survived that competition with those challenges.

Life is full of these competitions, which can allow us to thrive as a leader, or can put us into a place where we deny our inner leader, and struggle. The decision is up to you how you will respond in the competitions you face. Give yourself permission to take every opportunity that comes your way. There are individuals who have people that put them forward for promotion, or encourage them to start businesses for others. You just have to step forward in faith; you can do all things your inner mind, your subconscious mind, tells you—think it, write it down, formulate, and plan, and just do it.

The universe is good, and as you wake up each day, breathing and alert, be grateful; it is a new day, for new beginnings and your own individual marathon and race. You set the pace—what do you want to achieve? You can do it when you set your mind to it.

Still, recognise that competition can wear on us, mentally and physically. The result is that we might find ourselves doubting our ability to lead and to have our voices heard. With that in mind, let's focus on how caring for our mental health contributes to our ability to lead personally and professionally.

Mental Health Impacted by the Pandemic

During the 2008 financial crisis, employment changes highlighted the adverse impact on a range of chronic conditions, with the most substantial effect on mental health. In contrast, we are in unprecedented times (i.e., not necessarily comparable to the financial crisis), and evidence suggests that the COVID-19 pandemic significantly impacts mental well-being.

This unprecedented COVID-19 pandemic we have experienced globally, will have a short-term and long-lasting effect on society's mental health, from the complex interaction between diverse socio-economic determinants of health (Institute for Fiscal Studies, 2020). Having somewhere warm/safe to live and employment or running your own business are critical pillars for protecting and maintaining good mental health. However, it has become apparent that people have missed face-to-face human contact, an integral part of communication and mental well-being.

During the first wave of the pandemic, there were concerns regarding the economy and rising mental health needs, across private, public, and voluntary sectors. With the additional pressures experienced by many deemed essential workers, and changes for those managing a home and work-life balance, there was also the constant stress of worrying about being furloughed.

There is the spiritual saying, "Seek ye first the kingdom of God, and everything else will be added unto you." When you seek your union with the universe, and consciously accept the greater good, this law will give you faith, peace, and calm, despite worldwide chaos and instability. Tapping into our spirituality can also help to support our mental health. Leaders and coaches also find themselves in a unique position to give people tools to support good mental health, no matter what life throws at them.

As coaches and leaders, we can proactively develop mental health information and guidance for different people. Despite existing interventions and information available, there was a clear need for additional training for the wider workforce. Targeted coaching and mentoring, focused on leaders, individuals, and teams' strengths during these challenging times, can pay dividends for everyone's mental health.

Leading with Your Natural Gifts

Many people I coach express confusion regarding what their natural talents are and how they can lead effectively. Many of your talents might only surface if you try something new and pick it up really quickly. Others who try to pick up that same activity might need to practice for a long period, but may still never attain a high level of proficiency. Some individuals naturally grasp new things and excel, even if they are just told once or given a quick demonstration. However, there are times when your talents expose themselves to your interests and what brings you joy. Once you start exploring your interests and what inspires you, then your talents are more likely to float to the surface. Parents and schools play a very important part in identifying early strengths in children. I have spoken to many teachers and parents about this, and encourage them to focus on children's natural strengths and talents that the adults notice, and ask them to acknowledge these so that the children know what they are good at early in their lives.

Did I know what my talents and strengths were? I liked studying and was always taking first position and prizes in primary and secondary school from an early age. My father was an encourager and always encouraged me; however, when my father left the family home and left us in the care of my single mother, this was a great setback and had a negative impact on me. I suffered anxiety and I lost self-confidence, which impacted my schooling.

My mother continued to encourage me to focus on my education in spite of the challenges I faced, as I had become pregnant and then was a single mother at an early age. Fortunately, my mother remained a pillar of support throughout this difficult period. She told me that God is my father and provides everything I need. I held on to this belief throughout these challenging times. What my mother saw as my strength and talent of learning, paid dividends throughout my life. I have since completed my MBA, MA (DipSW), and BA (Hons) International Business and Economics, as well as a master's in neuro-linguistic programming, and training in psychotherapy without counselling training. I am also a mindfulness practitioner, a property investor, and a high frequency trader and (HFX) mentor. My gift was taking in information, processing it, and putting that to use. Ultimately, my talent aligned with my hard work, to equal success. No matter what your talents, without hard work and determination, they will not be able to take you to the next level of success. Discipline and unwavering focus on what you want and aspire to become is key to achieving your desired goal.

How you see yourself—either as talented and successful, or untalented and a failure—ends up determining the decisions you make, and thus shapes your reality, now and into the future. When you are coaching or being coached, it is vital that you explore your "perception of self," which is the way you view yourself, your genuine self-knowledge or varying degrees of distortion, attitudes, emotions, and other internal states. This helps you have a clear picture of who you perceive yourself to be.

Answering the question of who you perceive yourself to be can be challenging for some. Sensitivity and honesty with yourself is necessary. To improve your confidence, self-reflection unlocks a deeper understanding of who you are and how well you perform as a leader in different situations.

However, when you step out as a leader, how you perceive yourself can negatively impact how well you lead. Some of my clients sabotage themselves and have self-defeating behaviours by focusing on feelings of not belonging, which is known as imposter syndrome. Bear in mind, you are not the first person to suffer with these feelings. That is why having a coach helps you overcome these limiting beliefs and thoughts.

These feelings of inadequacy can persist, even when you are successful. Many of those looking to tap into leadership positions, find themselves suffering from chronic self-doubt and a sense of intellectual fraud, which overrides feelings of success or external proof of their competency. This challenge is one that is faced by women in particular.

How can you overcome this persistent challenge? Start by tapping into mindfulness. Recognise that not knowing everything does not make you a fraud; it just means that you have to delegate. When you do fail, reframe it as a learning experience. Most importantly, have self-compassion. Often, our inner dialogue can be harder on us than is really necessary.

Another way to combat feelings of inadequacy is to examine who is in your inner circle. The people surrounding you have a phenomenal impact on your life. Your mind is like a garden; it needs nurturing through positive and constructive thoughts. Today's daily news is often infused with negative stories and divisive thoughts, which add to the unprecedented times of the COVID-19 lockdown that started in March 2020. Streamlining the human mind is based upon the fundamental truth that what a man thinks is what he becomes.

As a leader, you are not just putting up fake positivity, but you are also focusing on faith, goodness, the greater good, and expanding your consciousness. Conservation of stillness allows you to speak life into situations and manifest good things now and into the future, thus shaping your reality.

Enjoy the goodness within you as a leader. Many of us do not know how to respond to our thoughts, allowing them to lead us down a dark path of negativity. I encourage you to read the story of Jesus Christ, in the Bible—how he formed a team of disciples who had different strengths and talents, the way he dealt with disputes, and his unwavering focus on his goal. His mentoring and leadership are inspiring. You will be encouraged.

Research has suggested that environment is often more important than heredity. The people we are surrounded by have a greater bearing on your life and your success than what is built in the genes. While there is some genetic conditioning that impacts how we approach the world, the truth is that our environmental conditioning has a much broader impact on our quality of life. By improving your thinking, you will then attract a different group of people into your life. That will change your environment as they add a fresh perspective to your life. Seek to network with people who are doing what you want and aspire to achieve.

Their thinking will influence your own thinking. Take a look at the five people you spend the most time with, and ask yourself, "If I had children, would I want them to grow up like these individuals?" If the answer is no, then you had better look for ways to change those five individuals that you spend the most time with. If your answer is yes, then you already have the right circle, one that is striving to push you to be the best you possibly can be.

What are the qualities in yourself that you want to amplify? I cannot overemphasise the need for you to look for individuals who already personify those qualities, and make an effort to spend time with them to deepen your relationship. They will influence you to develop those qualities even further. The people we're surrounded with have a phenomenal impact on our lives, and help to define who we are.

Perhaps you recognise that within your top five, there are toxic relationships that sabotage your ability to lead successfully in a variety of situations. Therefore, be honest with yourself about the toxic aspects of these relationships. The first person you lead is you. That level of honesty can help you identify the areas where you can initiate change.

Why is the bucket concept helpful during this process of understanding your relationships and their impact on your environment? The concept of a full or empty bucket gives understanding to the motivation behind behaviour. When our buckets are full, then we are much more inclined to fill our individual buckets and the buckets of others. On the other hand, when our buckets are empty, we tend to find ourselves struggling, wanting to dip into other people's buckets to just keep moving forward. Therefore, it is important to take the steps and surround yourself with people who help to fill up your buckets and energise you. Your focused action today, no matter how small, is bringing you towards your desired goal.

Before you can make any dramatic changes to your relationships and environment, you need to address your health in a variety of areas, particularly physical, mental, and spiritual.

Reflection Notes

Master Key 3

Balanced Lifestyle Paradigm

3

"A time for everything: A time to relax and a time to be busy, a time to frolic and a time to labour, a time to receive and a time to give, a time to begin and a time to finish."
– Jonathan Lockwood Huie

Health and well-being are of paramount importance and can be described as the achievement of physical fitness, mental well-being, and a combination of physical, social, intellectual, and emotional factors.

Your health plays a key role in balanced leadership on all levels. As such, it is a master key to fully unleash your inner leader.

The value of your health and well-being cannot be underestimated. Good health is your currency to achieve your goals and dreams. Therefore, investing in your health is investing in your future.

One of the main ways to influence your health is how and what you eat. Everything that we take into our bodies impacts how we function. If your diet is full of processed foods full of ingredients that you cannot pronounce, then it is likely to show in a lack of energy, unhealthy looking skin, and other physical problems.

Consider what you are eating as part of your daily routine, and how it is impacting your physical health. Making changes in your eating habits is unlikely to be easy, because so much of it is based upon the habits that you created and followed for years. In Chapter 1, I focused on the importance of discipline. When it comes to changing your eating habits and diet, discipline is even more critical. The main evidence-backed timeframe for habit breaking comes from 2009 research, which suggests it takes anywhere from 18 to 254 days. This research looked at 96 adults who wanted to change one specific behaviour. One person formed a new habit in just 18 days, but others needed more time (healthline.com).

Think of your body like a beautiful luxury car. It requires the high-octane gasoline to run at an optimal level. Yet instead of putting in the high-octane fuel, you opt for the 87 octane because it costs less. Over time, how do you think that car is going to perform? More problems are likely, simply because you are not investing in the right fuel.

Your body is that luxury car. It needs a high-octane diet, one that fuels it effectively. When you have a cheaper diet, one that focuses less on providing the right minerals, vitamins, and nutrients, then your body will perform just like the car, and problems will arise.

As a leader/coach and coachee, it is vital that you think deeply about not putting the wrong food in your mouth. Do your homework to learn more about plant-based foods and what your body needs, and make sure that your food choices are filling those needs effectively. When you demonstrate a willingness to make a change for the better, then as a leader, you have the power to influence others in a meaningful way.

Throughout the lockdown and quarantines during the COVID-19 pandemic, many of us found ourselves eating to cope with our feelings of frustration, stress, and anxiety. Our bodies reflected those poor eating habits, based not on what our bodies needed, but more on our mental and emotional needs in the moment. Discipline is key to finding new ways to cope with these challenges.

As a leader and coach, I draw attention to your habits, particularly those that directly impact your physical health. My goal is to get you to look with fresh eyes at how your habits could be negatively impacting your physical well-being. I won't lay out one specific eating plan for everyone, because our individual beliefs and physical needs are all different. Therefore, it is critical that you invest the time to learn how your eating habits and diet might need to be adjusted to bring your physical and mental health into alignment.

My sisters and I owned a restaurant and sandwich bar in North London. Due to its location, our customers represented a diverse slice of humanity. For instance, we had Jewish customers with unique dietary restrictions based upon their faith. Others had dietary needs based on specific physical conditions or lifestyle choices. Meeting their needs meant having a diverse offering available.

It also involved a great deal of planning. For our Jewish customers, we ordered kosher food. Regardless of whether they were English, Turkish, Greek, Polish, or Afro-Caribbean, we did our best to ensure that our customers' needs were met.

I used to drive a diesel transit van; it was part of my journey to the wholesale shops. During one of our commercial retail buying journeys, before I reached one of them, I saw that the gas tank was almost empty. I drove into the gas station. In my rush to get diesel into the tank and be on my way, I didn't pay attention to which nozzle I grabbed.

Within ten minutes, that lack of concentration resulted in the van making a funny noise and stopping. The engine would not start. I contacted a road service, and an experienced mechanic was dispatched. After asking a few questions and checking the van over, he pointed out that I had put in the wrong fuel. The van required draining, flushing, and refuelling before it would run properly. My rushing and lack of concentration ended up leaving me with a large bill to correct my mistake, and it essentially ended my shopping trip for the day.

If you are not concentrating on what you put into your body, you could be grabbing the wrong fuel nozzle, and will end up creating a roadblock to your success as a leader.

As a leader, coach, or coachee, the type of food you choose to eat determines your energy levels. Today, there are plenty of foods available, but not all of them have the same health benefits. In fact, many of them actually can be harmful if ingested regularly. According to the UN, bacon, ham, and sausages are among the most carcinogenic substances. Imagine that your ham sandwich is in the same league as cigarettes, alcohol, arsenic, and asbestos[1].

When coaching my clients, I point out how their food choices can impact whether they are healthy and balanced, while increasing and boosting their energy levels. Unfortunately, poor food choices can have the opposite effect, and your health will suffer. You can have all the money and opportunities in the world, but if you are not mindful about what you eat, then you compromise your health and limit your ability to lead effectively.

How can you determine if you are eating the right foods? Do your homework and research the options available in your area. Once you make mindful decisions to eat better, then your example can impact those around you. Recognise that you can also have a powerful impact by purchasing local foods that are in season. That can allow you to maximize the health benefits of fresh foods all year round.

Now that we have discussed the importance of diet, let's talk about how your physical health is impacted by your activity level. Are you active every day? COVID-19 obstructed our ability to get and stay active, because many of us were doing everything from home. I encourage my clients to incorporate

---

[1] https://www.theguardian.com/society/2015/oct/26/bacon-ham-sausages-processed-meats-cancer-risk-smoking-says-who

habits that get them moving, even if it is just a walk around your home. Find ways to get active, and be creative. Doing so will make it easier for you to stay active as life returns to normal. Plus, your habits will serve as an example to your family, encouraging them to make healthier choices as well. Discipline is necessary to create good habits for diet and exercise, but the benefits to your health and energy levels are worth the effort.

Getting Financially Healthy

"There's health, wealth, love and happiness, and you gotta have all of em."
– Tai Lopez

When we talk about health, many of us focus immediately on our physical, mental, or emotional health. Rarely do we talk about the financial imbalances in our lives that negatively affect our ability to lead successfully.

Good financial management is essential to achieving your dreams and goals. After all, if you have limited resources, it can be difficult to achieve anything. When you are worrying about your finances, that can also negatively impact your ability to lead professionally and personally. It is vital that you have good financial management to successfully engage as a leader in all areas of your life. Teaching children from an early age to learn this skill, empowers them as future leaders to think about saving, investments, responsible forex and stock trading, life insurances and home insurances, to name a few, thus not leaving financial awareness till late in life, resulting in financial stress. Research shows that:

- 86% of employees say they spend time worrying about financial matters.
- 53% sometimes or always run out of money by the end of the month.
- 82% don't know if they will have enough money to retire with[2].

Do you fall into any of those categories? Concerns about your finances could influence your choices and reduce your ability to take advantage of opportunities to achieve your goals. Leading in your finances can open up your chances to advance your career and foster better relationships with your loved ones and co-workers.

Early in my career, I found myself in a situation where my finances were dictating my life. I was a single mother, working on my first degree. Even after I graduated and started working full time, I still found myself struggling financially. When I reflect back on that time, I realise that my spending was negatively impacting my financial health. My spending on items I could have done without, put me in a negative financial position. For instance, I was frequently shopping to create a wardrobe that matched the seasonal trends. I was convinced I needed to look the part to succeed professionally, and that meant dressing expensively.

---

[2] bippit.com/financial-awareness

Money that I could have invested in a way to provide for my future, was being flitted away on clothes that I just wore for a few months, and then they collected dust in the back of my closet. Over time, I realised that creating a working wardrobe helped me to stick with specific items, instead of just shopping every season.

As I work with clients, I challenge them to think about how they are managing their finances, and where they are putting their paycheque. Coaching goes beyond mentoring, so I help them to get honest about their spending and saving. Here are a few areas that you should consider as you focus on your financial health, both now and into the future.

- Do you have an insurance policy?
- Do you have multi-streams of income?
- Have you thought about property investments?
- Have you considered learning to trade stocks and shares? There is a risk you may lose money, but learning about the markets is important for making investments that match your risk levels.
- Do you know about the significant changes happening in the world, and how China's, India's, and Russia's economies could impact your financial investments?
- Should you or all children learn to speak the Mandarin, Spanish, or Russian languages? Being bilingual in our shrinking global community can be seen as a critical skill, particularly for younger generations.
- Considering your income now, how much money do you have for incidentals?

- Do you have a 6 to 12-month emergency fund, in case things go wrong with your business or if you lost a job?
- Do you have a 6-month, 12-month, 2-year, 5-year, or 10-year plan? Have you added these numbers to your current age to understand what your financial needs might be at these times in your life?
- What do you want to have achieved in a year, 2 years, 5 years, or a 10-year period? What financial moves do you need to make to have the resources to achieve those goals?

It seems harsh, but having financial freedom is key to doing the things you enjoy, and pursuing activities that inspire you or contribute to your legacy of leadership. When you look at your finances, be honest with yourself about every aspect, and be open to learning and applying essential financial principles to build your wealth and give yourself more opportunities to lead.

Maintaining Your Spiritual Well-Being

Think about those times of stress or when you faced a particular challenge in your life. Most of us reach out to a higher power, recognising our connection with the universe and how we belong to something greater than ourselves. It becomes a source of strength, courage, and purpose during times when we might be confused or hurting because of the actions of others.

Part of my coaching involves helping you to tap into your spirituality and the strength that it gives you. Hypnosis, mindfulness, and NLP are incorporated in helping you take time for your spiritual side, and it involves factoring in time every day for prayer, meditation, and reflection. Your relationship with God and the universe will help you develop deeper and more meaningful relationships with those around you. As a leader, when you can take time to centre yourself, then you bring your best to working and personal relationships. Developing spiritual disciplines helps you to connect and ground yourself spiritually.

"You can't truly be considered successful in business if your home life is in shambles."
– Zig Ziglar

That spiritual grounding also impacts your leadership skills. You demonstrate better attitudes, more stable emotions, good thoughts, and kindness to those on your team, which is likely to be mirrored by others. That also ripples out from yourself to affect your relationships and community, as well as the human race. In times of distress, you can tap into your divine connection and draw strength from God and the universe.

Personally, I have developed a routine that includes one hour of focused prayer, meditation, and gratitude time. I take a few minutes to write down what I am grateful for, and then take the time to reflect on these things daily. It is also important to challenge myself to find different things to be grateful for, thus helping me to be more mindful throughout the day. Throughout the day, I also make a point to express gratitude throughout my daily tasks. This practice will shift your focus and perception of the world, thus giving you a positive mindset (Mindset Of Excellence: Think and Grow Rich and Believe In Yourself)and contributing to your spiritual well-being. I also take time to pray for other people. My mother always taught us to pray for teachers, nurses, doctors, the police, pilots, and friends and family, to name a few. Make your own prayer list. This removes the focus from yourself, to acknowledge what other people do to make the world a better place.

Building up Your Relationships

Leading means connecting with others on a variety of levels. To get the best out of people, including creativity and innovation, you need to know those people on your team at a deeper level beyond their name. Get to know their talents and strengths. Find out what their goals are and how you can align their goals with the larger goals of the organisation.

Coaching, as part of your leadership, involves establishing what individuals are working on and where they can be most effective. Establishing peer-to-peer relationships is key to an individual worker's day-to-day interactions and productivity. That productivity ultimately sets them up to be successful in meeting the organisation's goals.

Relationships with managers and other leaders can also be nurtured, especially through coaching and mentoring, which can help your team to develop more of their hidden talents. Employees may worry about top-down feedback. Therefore, encourage them to pay attention to input from their peers, and to be open to giving it when asked. Feedback is how growth happens, but if relationships are not developed with this idea of improvement, then individuals might hesitate to share critical information. Here are some questions to consider, both as a leader and as someone who is part of a team:

- What do your teammates think of you?
- How do they feel about the work they are doing?
- What do they believe they could improve upon?
- In regard to your teams, are there clear directions set, and are those directions constantly being reinforced?
- Do they understand what they are doing?

Never assume that people have understood what is required of them; everyone has a different learning or communication style. People can be either visual, kinaesthetic, or audio learners; therefore, always have different ways of communication.

If they were off on something, discussions should involve communicating how to correct their course and get back on track. Avoid contributing to a blame culture, one that will end up increasing the negativity in the workplace, while also decreasing productivity. Effective relationships are based on clear communication, and defining roles in a way that everyone understands. Confusion leads to blame and counterproductivity, which can be detrimental to achieving your goals and leading your team successfully.

Coping with Change by Embracing the Warrior Within

Each of us has a different reaction to change. Some of us focus on the negative aspects of change, while others tend to focus on the positive aspects of change. Regardless, it is important to recognise that change is necessary for growth. Without changes, we cannot learn, explore, or create. Our journey as a leader will become stagnate. The COVID-19 lockdown brought about radical change for organisations, families, and individuals. Everyone has had to learn to cope with this change, and we all continue to cope with unprecedented changes.

With that in mind, let's talk about the value of time as it relates to change. Those of us who are younger might not have a full appreciation of the gift of time. After all, we feel invincible, and it seems as if we have years to accomplish all of our dreams and goals. As we age, however, our perspective of time begins to shift. Now we recognise the importance of prioritising our days to maximize our productivity. We reach milestones and realise that some dreams or goals might be out of reach. Having said that, by having faith backed with action, you can do all things in alignment with the universe. All things are possible.

My mother used to say, "If only I could be a child again," and, "If I knew then what I know now." My sisters, brothers, and I used to just shrug this off. Little did I know that as an adult, I would utter those same phrases.

Bearing that in mind, think about the wisdom you have already achieved based upon your previous experiences. Likely, it was the result of change. The challenge is to not delay change but to embrace it. Since time (every 24 hours) is a precious commodity, there is a saying: "Time is money." It is essential that we see change as a way to shift into a new direction and get the most out of our lives. Leading with a perspective where change is a gift and a blessing, can allow you to assist others to embrace change as well.

Once you recognise the power of change, then you can use it to create opportunities and open more doors—not just for you but for members of your team. However, there are also ways that change can be used to break bad habits or to end toxic relationships, in either business or personally.

I learned about the importance of creating change when I opted to travel for a period of time. My insurance policies were put on automatic debit, along with other payments. I hired an estate manager, whose job was to collect the rents from my properties and put them into the account. Then as the debits came out, the funds would be available. Imagine my surprise to find out that he not only had not done that, but because the funds were not available, all my payments had been declined by the bank, and my policies had been cancelled. What was even worse was that I had the money to pay the premiums for the policies for an entire year, but I had opted to go the route of payments. It ended up costing me much more in terms of getting everything straightened out with my insurance agents and tenants. My leadership was lacking, and it had a financial cost. Why is this important? Because how you lead is going to directly impact every aspect of your life, including your finances and relationships. When you plan ahead, show compassion, and embrace clear communication, then you develop as a leader, becoming someone that others trust to lead them through major changes.

As a leader, you will face setbacks. When I speak of the "warrior within," it is because that warrior is your well of courage and strength to face the unhealthy aspects of your life and get them in order. It gives you the necessary tools to create or accelerate changes in your life. The result is that your inner leader is able to flourish, no matter the challenges or obstacles that might show up in your path. Remember that as you build up your spiritual health, you will see that you are not alone. God, the universe, and many other individuals are all there to help you, to fill your buckets when they are running low.

You sabotage yourself if you do not acknowledge your feelings, face your fears, and embrace your emotions, including doubts and uncertainty. As a leader, you will feel these things, but it is essential that you do not let these feelings handicap you from achieving what your talents can bring to life. When you struggle, ask for help. Leaders do not need to go it alone. Real leadership is recognising both your strengths and weaknesses, while reaching out to others and tapping into their strengths to foster growth.

As a leader, how you cope with change will set the example for your team. If you see someone struggling with the changes in your organisation, meet with them, and reassure them about confidentiality. Talk about what they are scared of and what is making them fear this change. If you can work through it with them, then they will buy in and help others to embrace the changes. As each team member feels valued, they become stronger and, ultimately, the team remains strong.

One of the biggest changes in any organisation is the old school versus the next generation. As technology drives our world to new achievements, organisations must find a way to foster leadership that embraces the talents of multiple generations. Leaders and coaches must be mindful of generational differences within organisations, bearing in mind that the age group of 18 to 35—the millennial generation—as employees and managers, has changed the business landscape globally. They find conforming to the traditional ways of working or doing things as being difficult. This presents a challenge to those of previous generations.

The millennials challenge the status quo; they are not passive, or respectful of leaders, as they do not take orders quietly as older generations did. They question and want to know the reason why things are being done or proposed to be done, which is a good thing. The expectations of millennials is to be involved every step of the way, and as part of teams. The millennials are not as committed as previous generations were, where they held on to jobs, for life, in one organisation. Millennials want to participate, and they want to be nurtured. They question organisational values and ethics in relation to climate change, responsible management, child labour policies, and authenticity. Millennials want flexible working conditions, and open and creative workspaces.

Leaders of today must understand that millennials have a different way of receiving instructions and being motivated, if pushing them to work hard, to improve, and to grow with the organisation. For this reason, the approach is to treat each person as having leadership qualities. Their participation in organisational/business growth, as a key stakeholder, is key. The changing and revolving of employees, if they are empowered and motivated, and are given the opportunity to excel and take on responsibilities within the company, encourages and motivates them, and provides them every opportunity to succeed and be rewarded.

Leaders and coaches must be mindful that the "one hat fitting all," does not necessarily mean to be equally rewarded financially. It may sound strange, but for some millennials, all they may want is recognition and acknowledgement. It is up to their manager to understand what motivates them to realise their potential.

With that in mind, let's talk about what your inner leader can bring to your team and the organisation as a whole.

Reflection Notes

Master Key 4

Lead Individuals and Teams to Excel

4

When it comes to coaching or mentorship, the first thing that most people tend to think of is how they can show up their weaknesses. In fact, they often spend so much time focusing on those weaknesses that their strengths tend to atrophy from a lack of use. Often, the most important thing to recognise about a weakness is that someone else can be strong in that area. Instead of spending your time and energy to improve slightly in one weakness or another, I challenge my clients to excel in their strengths. Whatever they are good at, needs to be their focus. Use it to benefit yourself and others on your team.

One of the best methods to capitalise on strengths, and shift everyone's focus, is to create mentoring or coaching teams within your organisation. Think of them as the means to identify strengths, and the resources to capitalise on them, at a team and organisational level. As an accredited strengths coach, helping teams with tools like Team Strengths Grid, gives team members a way to visualise their collective.

To tap into my own strengths, I spent over $50,000 in self-development courses and trainings. I made it my goal to surround myself with a great network of people, who challenged me to take risks and aspire for great things. In building your mentoring or coaching teams, focus on adding the individuals that inspire others, and cheer them on. These coaches and mentors need to be practical in helping individual team members, rather than as a team, to set goals, while pushing them to reach outside of their comfort zone.

Along the way, focus on bringing in a diverse group of individuals to lead this effort. Why do you want diversity in your teams? It allows you to bring in the broadest possible amount of experiences and skills. Mentors and coaches are sharing their experiences even as they work with others to capitalise on their own.

The individuals on these teams provide a natural sounding board for the different team members within your organisation. While I focused initially on the inner leader that we all have, I also recognised how important it is to be inclusive. Organisations around the world face challenges and obstacles to growth as part of their industry. Interestingly, the solution could be right in front of the management, but they do not see it because the leadership voices are limited to just one or two people.

Diversity and inclusion are not just buzzwords but reflect a way to lead. It involves looking to hear from a variety of voices, capitalising on their experiences and knowledge. Your inner leader is strong and capable, but humility and integrity can help you to recognise that your knowledge does not encompass every topic or potential solution.

Leading your team should also involve taking whatever actions necessary to make sure people feel comfortable expressing themselves. I have coached many leaders who focus more on making demands than mining their team's strengths and using them effectively. Coaching as a leader means putting your team first and acknowledging the answers they hold inside themselves. It is up to you to demonstrate a willingness to allow those answers to come out.

That being said, not everyone is eager to voice their opinions or to speak up during group meetings. They might feel intimidated by others in the room. Diverse generations can also clash about what is protocol within these meetings. For instance, an older team member might find it unusual or disrespectful if a younger team member speaks up without being called on by the individual leading the meeting. They believe in a pecking order, which can lead to ideas being stifled.

Younger generations are inherently more tech savvy, simply because of how much technology is interwoven into their lives. Tap into that strength, and do not assume that just because they do not have experience in other areas, that they cannot be a source of strength for your team. Plus, you can give them opportunity to lead in their areas of strength and expertise, creating a team of leaders, where individuals can give and take in a way that brings out everyone's best.

Therefore, as you lead meetings, make a point to do what is necessary to break through these types of barriers. It could involve setting the tone by making everyone contribute to the meetings, and then gradually allowing for the meeting to become more of a group discussion instead of being directed solely by you.

Diversity means acknowledging how different individuals can bring unique strengths to a team based upon their backgrounds. There are some individuals who might have come from a background with less financially, which can make them extremely creative regarding how to do a lot with a little. Encouraging them to speak up can positively impact the bottom line, as you discover more cost-effective methods to handle production.

As you can see, leading often does not mean being the only one to speak. Instead, it means taking time to actively listen and allow others to voice their creativity and innovation through potential solutions. The team will benefit from being able to hear other voices, as well as the chance to work more effectively with individuals from different generations and backgrounds. There is a power that can be found in demonstrating respect for others, even if you disagree with them.

Respecting others can also mean taking the time to speak with individuals one on one, especially if you need to give feedback regarding areas of improvement. Talking down to individuals that are a part of your team, whether in private or in public, can undermine the trust in your relationships. That can end up making it challenging for you to get the best from them, if they fear that you will berate them. With that in mind, let's talk about supervising and how it changed with the pandemic.

Supervision: Virtually and Face-to-Face

For many leaders and coaches, speaking with individuals face-to-face was part of how they led. After all, they could see faces, read body language, and interpret it to determine the best way forward. Now, with a shift towards video meetings, brought on by the pandemic, leaders and coaches are having to make significant changes to how they function in the age of virtual meetings.

That also means learning to trust those working from home that are not where you can supervise them directly. Building relationships is often key to maintaining your effectiveness as a leader, despite the challenges of having to lead within a virtual setting. For many leaders, that has involved regular check-ins with their staff on an individual basis. Micromanaging can stifle creativity and can make team members feel undermined, resulting in frustrations. Being open to hearing what their challenges are, and brainstorming ways to address them, can allow you to still get productivity out of your team, even during these difficult and challenging times. Most of your efforts are going to involve work you have likely already done without realising it. Simply put, you are tapping into the strengths of your team.

My framework of what the word "strengths" stands for is important to take into consideration in understanding principles of leadership, which I formulated in my MBA Management Research Projects 2020.

They are:

S Strengths
T Talents
R Relationships
E Excellence
N Non-negotiable (Claim your strengths and talents, and then invest in them.)
G Goal setting (Specific, Measurable, Attractive, Realistic, and Timeliness)
T Timeframe/Management
H Humanity (Be polite; your country is part of the world—accept differences, do good, be warm-hearted, be affectionate, and be inclusive. Also included here is well-being and a balanced lifestyle.)

When I have looked at teams, the above are different key elements you as a leader should keep applying and reflecting on. Both in local government and multinational companies, teams require bias blinders. The reality is that we all move through the world making judgments based upon the biases we carry. Simply put, being in the winning lane is depended on having the best team, with differing strengths and talents. I have worked in both the private sector and local government, helped run a family business, and have been involved in property investments and high frequency Forex trading. During all these different activities, I have observed that the best teams include more women. I encourage you to reflect on your own experience.

Being attuned to emotional intelligence is key in today's business landscape. A pair of 2010 studies examined collective intelligence in teams. They wanted to understand why some teams are "smarter" than the sum of their individual IQs. There are three sides to understanding this phenomenon. The most effective teams allow each individual to give their opinion rather than having the discussion dominated by one or two people. The individuals on those successful teams are better at reading complex emotional states, and they have more women on the team. This can be partly explained by the fact that women tend to be better at reading emotional states than men.

Strengths include leadership, communication, or writing skills. Common weaknesses include a fear of public speaking, imposter syndrome, a lack of experience with software or a program, or difficulty with taking criticism. Investing in self-development is key to building self-confidence and gaining new skills. Operating in a space of abundance is a choice.

In the main human resources landscape, the term "weakness" is regarded ethically inappropriate. Within these circles, individuals are now interpreted as having "strengths" and "opportunities," or "challenges"—but not "weaknesses." Some businesses are even planning to remove negative feedback (https://twitter.com/drtcp).

A lack of success in projects in organisations is due to objectives not being clear, not enough communication, senior management not supporting projects, inadequate scheduling, failure to pull together, and deciding processes of choosing brilliant ideas to pursue. This is the result of leaders and employees not having an understanding of their unique strengths and talents. Putting a project team together, without considering team member strengths, can reduce the profitability or return on investment of an organisation, simply because they are unlikely to have the right people in place to ensure success. Investing in management and team strengths assessments is key.

By putting aside focusing on weaknesses, and instead exploring the intricate details of team members' strengths, through taking the Clifton Strengths assessment, for example, can help to discover the various sources of strengths within your team members.

Talents are recurring patterns of thought, feeling, and behaviour. In other words, they are what come naturally to you when you operate in the flow. Whereas skills and knowledge quantify based upon past performance, talents quantify potential. Talents might include innovation, adaptability, persuasion, communication, teamwork, and mental strengths that are useful to a pursuit, profession, art, activity, or task. For example, in the current IA and internet-based business landscape, senior leaders should possess the skill to communicate directly with the tech guys and the engineers, even if they are engineering executives. Plus, the geeks would know they had the CEO's attention every week.

All of these efforts are based around building relationships within your organisation. To get the best from your team, you need to encourage relationship-building exercises. Relationship is the state of being related or interrelated. The relation is connecting or binding participants, such as through kinship.

Building relationships can lead your team to excellence. Unfortunately, it is not easy to do. Excellence is a quality that people appreciate because it can be challenging or hard to find. Excellence is the quality of excelling, providing a service at high level, consistently without slacking, and being truly the best at something. Getting an A+ shows excellence. Challenge yourself to do class A+ tasks and performance in every area of your life.

In looking at each of the above within the framework of a team, you must look at each aspect and reflect on what this means for you, and on the relevance to your leadership style, to understand how those you manage or that follow you can also apply them.

I acknowledge that coaching and mentoring individuals requires taking time to know those who work with you and for you, individually and also as teams. In addition, this effort requires your understanding of difference, diversity, and inclusion.

Greater diversity in the workforce leads to greater profitability, creativity, and further value creation. This formula applies to the executive level, as McKinsey found a statistically significant correlation between diverse leadership and better financial performance. For example, companies in the top quartile for ethnic diversity, at the executive level, are 33 per cent more likely to have above-average profitability than companies that are in the bottom quartile. For issues of gender diversity, companies in the top quartile are 21 per cent more likely to have above-average profitability than companies that are in the bottom quartile

(McKinsey 2018). However, do not be quick to assume that just checking boxes to hire specific individuals will give you diversity within your organisation or team. Instead, diversity involves hiring diverse backgrounds and then allowing them to share and contribute. They should not just be the token effort to appear diverse on brochures and in marketing. Make them feel like part of the team by building a relationship and making your team feel interconnected.

Successful relationships within the workplace are built upon a foundation of respect and trust. As a leader, you set the tone for your team by demonstrating respect for them. Even when you have to address potential issues, your tone and body language still need to be respectful of those around you.

Unfortunately, many leaders get a sense of entitlement, feeling that they are always in the right. That leads to power dynamics that can contribute to bullying. You can be so determined to put people into their place that you end up silencing members of your team altogether. They feel as if they are working to avoid coming in contact with you.

I encourage the leaders that I coach to focus on building their empathy muscles, allowing them to connect with their team. Having a sense of belonging is a critical part of the foundation for your team's success. Avoid jumping to the conclusion that everyone on your team requires being micromanaged by you. Instead, allow them to be successful. Leadership allows for a certain level of independence, but remember that it comes with accountability.

Additionally, everyone should know your organisation's brand and how their efforts are linked to building that brand. They are not just moving paper from one side of a desk to another. Your team members are contributing to growing your brand and burnishing its reputation. Even when they understand how they are critical to the success of your organisation, it can be challenging to be flexible.

Organisations today are often built upon a specific set of rules and processes. It becomes a bureaucracy that makes it difficult for your organisation to pivot when necessary, especially during critical or disruptive periods. Therefore, do not put processes into place that are so stuck in stone that you cannot be flexible. Instead, offer opportunities for change and adaptation. Give your organisations the mechanisms to be fluid, especially when big changes are happening within the industry.

That being said, employees should be comfortable making mistakes or failing from time to time, because that can often lead to ideas and processes that can increase profitability and productivity. A blame culture will have people trying to cover up mistakes instead of learning from them, and it will not foster positive results. Assist people to grow, as this will give them a sense of belonging.

Your efforts will contribute to creating a strong company culture. One of the biggest challenges facing leaders in our technology-driven world is managing a work-life balance. Our phones connect us with emails and work constantly. To foster an environment that allows your employees to recharge, make hours for replies and then stick to them. Not only will it be good for your family, it will also allow you to recharge as their leader. Many of the emails we receive in the evening are not emergencies that need a response right now. Recognise their work but also how important their time with their families is to keeping them productive. If you want your team to be excited to come to work, then give them time to unwind and recharge.

Finally, I encourage leaders to build a future for your organisation, both in environment and culture, that gets your team excited. They can see opportunities to grow within your organisation, which gives them a sense of purpose. Collaboration, diversity, and coaching can foster a culture that contributes to innovation and growth that puts your organisation at the top of your industry consistently.

Remember that no man is an island, and so you need to figure out how to collaborate and build connection with everyone on your team. With that in mind, let's talk about fostering creativity and managing change within a disruptive and constantly shifting global economy.

Reflection Notes

Master Key 5

Lead in Managing Change and Creativity

5

Never has there been a time when change has globally impacted the business world, like the unprecedented COVID-19 lockdown that began in March 2020. As I write this, countries are racing to vaccinate their populations, and businesses still feel the impact throughout global supply chains. The result was that businesses needed to adapt, organisations needed to shift, and everyone was introduced to schooling online or was left to fend for their children with no traditional education outlets available. Everything happened quickly and tested our ability to adapt. For many businesses, managing change is part of how they function in their industries, and so the platforms were there for adaptation.

Change management is the formal process for organisational change, including a systematic approach and application of knowledge. It means defining and adopting corporate strategies, structures, procedures, and technologies to deal with change stemming from internal and external conditions, according to the "Society for Human Resources Management, 2007 Change Management Survey Report."

Career leadership coaching today requires adjusting to meet the needs of leaders, employees, and organisations where these changes need to take place. As a leader and coach, you have to be creative, visionary, and forward thinking. Single-mindedness and focus are fundamental to keeping everyone on task, primarily if a change occurs in several stages. You need to remind them of the end goal, especially when it feels out of reach. For example, looking at case studies of visionary leaders of companies that are leading today can help you as a coach to draw examples to inspire or motivate your team. With that in mind, let's talk about the vital attributes of winners and how you model them for your team.

- Winners are always working hard.
- Winners are always focusing on the task at hand.
- Winners are always fighting to stay positive.
- Winners are always looking for the people and representatives to raise money in business or politics.
- Winners are consistently writing and reviewing plans.
- Winners are goal setters.
- Winners are in competition with themselves and with everybody.
- When the chips are down, winners never quit.

You are a winner as all of the above applies to you. Your journey to this day is that of a leader, a winner, and someone who can achieve their goals while embracing change.

When I coach, I encourage my coachees to embrace change in the global market. When I studied a module called Change and Creativity, for my MBA, this module opened my eyes. As a leader, you are aware that creativity in this landscape of artificial intelligence (AI) is the driving force of founders who lead thriving businesses, like Amazon and Elon Musk's companies, as drivers of change. For example, in 2020:

Ranking of the Companies, Ranked 1 to 100	**Market Capitalisation in Billion U.S. Dollars**
Alphabet (United States)	919.3
Facebook (United States)	583.7
Alibaba (China)	545.4
Tencent Holdings (China)	509.7

You must keep abreast of the technological changes happening worldwide, and strive to leverage your business to embrace, review, and implement change to suit the current COVID-19 landscape and beyond. As a coach and coachee, keep in mind that creativity drives innovation and change, and pushes individuals you work with to excel in a complex business world, which is uncertain, volatile, and full of ambiguity (CUVA).

Your understanding that failure leads to success is key. When I was studying for my MBA, there were modules I had to submit because I was not able to successfully complete them the first time. I did not give up. This gave me an opportunity to learn more and to gain more ideas; resubmitting essays and passing them taught me aspects of the modules I had not known. As a business owner, I have started businesses. For example, my sisters and I owned a sandwich bar and restaurant in North London. I also started a recruitment company, and I am a property investor and high frequency Forex trader. Did I make mistakes? I did, but I learnt so much. I drew strength from lessons learnt by other business founders who had also failed. People only do what you inspect, not what you expect. As a leader, coach, and coachee, keeping in mind the importance of monitoring systems, attention to detail, planning, and reviewing progress and programmes against deadlines, is key.

Have the confidence to challenge whatever happens—to perceive, to carry on, and to achieve set aims, goals, and objectives. Again, using agile working and project management tools pays dividends.

Addressing the "blame culture" is key. When I worked in social care, I was acutely aware of the negative media reports about social workers. I kept questioning and reminding myself why I had become a social worker, and focused on the difference I wanted to make in protecting vulnerable children who experience abuse (sexual, physical, psychological, modern-day slavery, and related traumas). That was my goal, and no matter the criticism, I knew my focus and did just that. I am proud of myself for following my passion concerning working in the field. I was safeguarding children, and then worked in adult services, with those who experienced cancer, dementia, Alzheimer's, area anxiety, grief, and loss.

I worked for two local authorities that went through a merger. Change, and the way employee engagement became apparent in the process, taught me that management needs to be timely, sensitive, and effective when communicating with employees. I learned a lot about the importance of communication and employee buy-in.

As a certified Agile practitioner, Agile today is regarded as one of the most popular approaches due to its flexibility and evolutionary nature. It started in 2001 with the Agile manifesto, and was originally made for software development. Over time, the Agile project management evolved and became a popular choice for many project managers, irrespective of the industry.

Agile, in a nutshell, is an iterative and incremental approach to project management that helps teams keep up with the demands of the modern workplace. It consists of different methodologies, and all of them are based on the concepts of flexibility, transparency, quality, and continuous improvement.

To get a free sheet of 9 Key Benefits of Using the Agile Methodology, log on to www.careerleadershipcoachingtoday.com

As a leader, coach, and coachee, it is vital to understand that failure inspires creativity, to gear themselves up for rapid technological change and creativity. This provides a requirement for strategic leadership in organisation, to prepare for radical change and creativity, with curious research and development teams rapidly exploring new product trials to remain profitable and competitive.

Discussion of traits in leadership should revolve around how you can foster work environments to view failure as learning, and digital skills as opportunities for automation, rather than blame and stifle creativity, which can be costly and result in bankruptcy or hostile takeovers. Examples will be given of companies, CEOs, and founders who failed but were able to learn from failure, leading to success. It is important that the benefits and the need for toolkits be adopted in order for companies to foster creative landscapes, to embrace disruptive technological changes and energy, and embed these in all teams. The Wired Life video referenced below outlines the impact of technological changes and creativity: https://youtu.be/LNZjm2u39MQ.

In career leadership coaching, the importance of failure in creativity and extension innovation (change) in organisations, as strategic leadership, is weighed down with accountability to maintain change and creativity in a complex business environment, where disruptive technologies are continually changing at break-neck speed. For strategic leaders to have a transparent, non-blaming culture, with confident and motivated employee engagement that embraces changing disruptive technologies, and maintains low employee turnover from the millennial generation, is challenging.

"Those who care to fail miserably can achieve greatly."
– John F. Kennedy

Failure should be our teacher, not our undertaker. Failure is delay, not defeat. It is a temporary detour, not a dead end. In the end, avoiding failure means doing nothing, saying nothing, and producing nothing. Be anxious for nothing, and continue to strive to complete what you planned to do. Whether it is studying for a course, running a business, training for a marathon or a swim race, sticking to an exercise regime, or making a commitment to eat a more plant-based diet, they are your goals, and you are the chief executive of your life. Motivate yourself, and do what you were born to do. Have the passion and commitment to finish what you started. Do not be distracted. There is a saying: "Try, try, try again, and if at first you do not succeed, try again." You will make it. Seek the services of a coach. As a strengths coach, I have helped women and men—property investors, landlords, students, teams, and entrepreneurs—to focus on individual and organisational objectives and turnover. I am also passionate about parents, caregivers, schools, and organisations developing future leaders through strengths based on focused teaching and training.

"If you are not prepared to be wrong,
you will never come up with anything original."
– Ken Robinson

The definitions of change and creativity must be understood. Change is to do something differently, and fostering creativity is the ability to turn innovative and inventive thoughts and ideas into genuine, unique inventions or products. Being creative is typified through the talent to see the ecosphere in a disruptive and contemporary manner, by exploring and discovering unknown designs to unconnected portents, managing to create new technologies or solutions.

Culture and Space

I have personally experienced stress, often I needed some space to reflect on my thoughts and recharge. When I was studying my MBA programme, it was fascinating that my lecturer, on the module of change and creativity, encouraged creative space and thinking outside the box about spaces that inspire inspiration. He arranged for the whole cohort to visit the Tate Morden Gallery (https://www.tate.org.uk/whats-on/tate-modern/exhibition/olafur), away from the lecture rooms, to provide an opportunity for us to experience a creative reflective space. In other organisations, the whole team could have a team away day to bond and have creative space to discuss projects. This can help inspire individuals, away from the usual restrictive office space, to tap into their creativity and find inspiration. Even napping on the job is something that is no longer sniffed at, to give employees rest time to foster creativity. According to a 2008 survey from the National Sleep Foundation, 34% of U.S. companies allow naps during breaks at work. Some offices even have designated nap pods or nap rooms. At Google, nap pods are available to employees looking for a private place to snooze. These nap pods are shaped like the Pac-Dots that Pac-Man eats.

I have previously arranged and ran weekend retreats in Dorset, for leaders and individuals who want to have time away from the hustle and bustle of everyday business life. These retreats give them access to open natural spaces, the sea, and the sandy beaches in Dorset; and feedback from attendees has been very positive. Unfortunately, because of the challenges that the COVID-19 lockdown landscape brought about—a problem for all of us, nationally and internationally—such events have not been run.

Creativity cannot be slotted into boxes as leaders/clients/ teams seek to find solutions. Organisations need to foster an open approach for anyone in the organisation to access training, which is inclusive of all departments as creative. "Change ideas" can come from anyone. Each individual is a leader in their own right.

Artificial intelligence is quickly developing, and the progression of the conceivable outcome of "robots" and technologies on human lives is beginning to manifest, and it is not science fiction or futuristic. Getting to this stage has required trials, failures, and successes.

Leadership and Creative Leadership

The leader who presents as a servant who looks to serve and encourage others, is viewed as able to drive inspiration and creativity, and instill a collaborative landscape (Greenleaf (1977). The idea is connected to strategic leadership, which is creative (Freement, Isaksen, and Doval, 2002). Academic contributions to the supportive landscape include Tagiuri and Litwin, 1968, Litwin and Springer, 1967. Some academics, such as Talbot, Cooper and Barrow (1992); Amabile, Conti al (1996); and Turnipseed (1994), contest that a range of participation among teams who are allowed the space to engage on a day-to-day basis of coming up with creative ideas and timeframes to achieve these is key to success. This type of environment, provided by strategic, collaborating leadership, instills and allows a dynamic, motivated, energetic, and creative workforce that also achieves work and lifestyle balance. They feel valued and involved in current and future organisational aims and goals.

Additionally, freedom and independence is the level at which team members are allowed to be creative, have autonomy, and work in the absence of continued monitoring and the seeking of approval from senior management for decisions.

Strategic leadership provides openness and trust in the work environment, and provides safety of team members' emotional relationships. Team members feel free to be honest and are able to give respectful, professional, constructive contributions without the fear of being blamed. They can acknowledge the efforts and creative ideas of others, explore new avenues, options, and opportunities, and take ownership and responsibility of tasks.

Research shows disturbing heights of not only job disruption but the landscape of how disruptive technologies are affecting everyday life, in both a positive and—to those who have not embraced technology—a negative way. Two years ago, Kai-Fu Lee predicted that artificial-enabled machines would replace more than fifty percent of jobs occupied by people, in a short space of the next ten years. Disruptive technology is impacting business viability and daily lives. IA and technology are here to stay. The diagram below shows the creative value of IA.

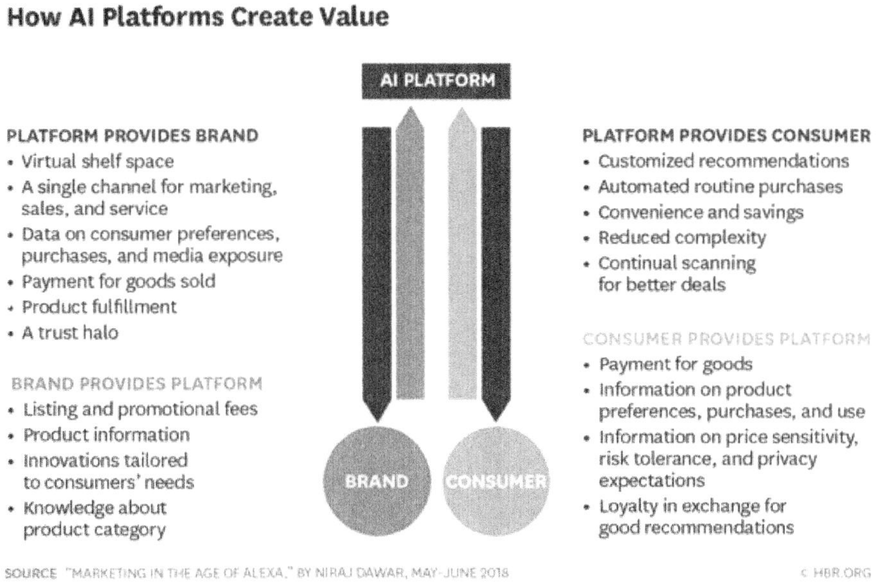

Tushman and Nader (1986) note "the importance of innovation—the process during which leap-changes are effected—is generally recognised. More than ten years ago, we already predicted that managing innovation would become the most important organisational task of the future. However, as companies strive to keep abreast and create new innovations, failure is part of the process."

Design Thinking Performance and Storytelling

Henry Ford depicts a story of trial and failure, which inspired creativity.

"Failure is simply the opportunity to begin again, this time more intelligently."
– Henry A. Ford
(Google.com)

Prior to succeeding, Ford faced significant failures at the time he initially produced "his first automobile." Those providing him funding developed doubts. He could not secure monitory support to design and manufacture his two automobile start-ups. However, to become a successful inventor and entrepreneur, Ford capitalised the mistakes and failings he made, as teachings as well as instructions, to inform his inventions (www.googlescholar).

I have made mistakes too. When I have failed, I have picked myself up and kept trying. Failure is necessary, but at times, failure resulted from a lack of supervision. At times, it has been the people I have trusted to carry out responsibilities that I should have inspected. I feared falling into the bad habit of micromanaging, but the results of not effectively managing were costly. I ended up closing down my recruitment business. I was paying a recruitment consultant—£30784 per annum, at £2565 per month—but placements were not made timely, and I lost the business. It was not a problem to them because they were still getting paid. They carried on with their lives, and I suffered the consequence. I can now help clients not suffer the same costly mistakes that I made. Do not rush to trust people. Do not be emotional. Take time and be rational, with clarity of the benefits and evidence that show employee commitment to meet set goals and objectives. Review daily, weekly, and monthly to ensure that time and money are not wasted.

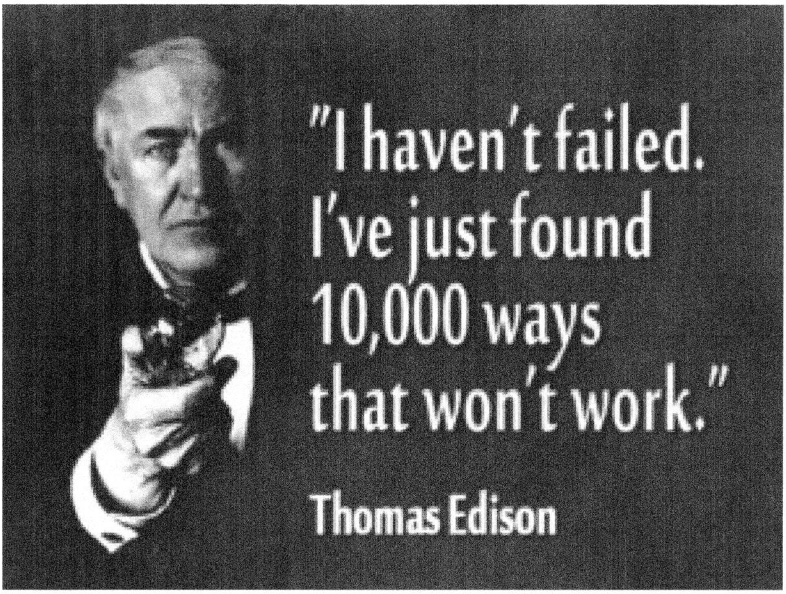

Another famous example is Thomas Edison, one of the most acknowledged inventors, who queried and asked about anything the failing exposed. He willingly noted what he learned. His recordings have factual information of his education from the trials. Once, an assistant asked why he continued to persevere efforts to develop an ongoing wire "for the light bulb," despite failing on 1000 occasions. His explanation was that he could not comprehend the helper's questioning. Edison's mental reasoning was that he had not failed once. He told the helper that he had learned 1000 things that had not worked. Edison ultimately finished his "Patent 251,539 for the light bulb that ensured his fame and fortune." (https://thinkjarcollective.com)

It is interesting that in Britain, the business landscape individuals are reluctant to discuss their failures, compared to the U.S., where failure is accepted with positivity, and a lot of individuals will essentially fail to achieve success. The Apple story is inspiring. In the early days, Apple was on the brink of failure. Now the organisation is valued in excess of £267bn (1 trillion U.S. $). The people who embrace the lessons of failure are the ones who go on to succeed (cityam.com).

Leading Creative Change

Success and failure are guaranteed to occur in organisations as they strive to develop new ideas to remain competitive and profitable. Trial and error is a web entwined, organisational leadership culture and teamwork. Smith (1996) described a team as "a small number of people with complementary skills, who are mutually committed to a common purpose, a common set of performance goals, and a commonly agreed upon working approach."

Creative change means acknowledging what no longer works, and being open to doing things in a new way, with a new direction and fresh perspective. It is not always easy, especially if your organisation has been leading the industry for years. Yet if your organisation is not growing and changing, then it is stalling and will eventually fail.

The building industry has also been faced with a lot of change with the demands in property, which can lead to shortcuts in building construction. It is therefore imperative that focus is continually maintained within all aspects of the construction process to ensure full compliance of building regulations, and that best construction practices are maintained. Even though there have been advances and changes in the building construction technologies, it is still imperative that change, creativity, and focus is maintained. The same dedicated approach is necessary to be applied in property management.

Experimenting and exploring new technologies and projects can present challenges to accept failure, for strategic leadership and, in turn, for employees not to be afraid to acknowledge failure, without fear of being blamed. Thinking of strategic leaders as saviours can be a suitable excuse for employees who leave in fear of blame.

Organisations need to motivate staff to spearhead, to be bold enough to explore ideas, and to seek solutions for problems that disruptive technologies are presenting. But, again, the personality factor contributes hugely to foster a creative work environment.

Trait	Description
Openness	Curious, original, intellectual, creative, and open to new ideas
Conscientiousness	Organized, systematic, punctual, achievement oriented, and dependable
Extraversion	Outgoing, talkative, friendly, and enjoys being in social situations
Agreeableness	Affable, tolerant, sensitive, trusting, kind, and warm
Neuroticism	Anxious, irritable, temperamental, and moody

In today's internet-based business world, influential and expert strategic leadership in organizations, inspiring creativity, is needed. For example, tech titans Apple, Amazon, Google, Airbnb, Uber, Facebook, and Reddit (FT.com) continue to grow due to bold futuristic project planning. With this growth for these companies comes worker-related responsibilities: to offer pensions to gig workers in the gig economy, and those workers are eligible for a pension in order to have a decent standard of living in retirement. Thinking and planning of your insurance policies, investments, retirement, and family financial health is important.

On the other hand, the opposite landscape of traditional businesses, including M&S, Debenhams, and House of Fraser, has lagged and is trying to catch up to embrace disruptive technology, and pursue constant innovation of products and services technology. The companies with traditional models have been struggling to keep the businesses profitable, and to realise stakeholder return on investments since the turbulent 1990s. Businesses that lag in embracing change and creativity have suffered significantly, especially after the COVID-19 lockdown.

Why then is failure analysis often underplayed? First, examining our failures in depth is emotionally unpleasant and can chip away at our self-esteem. Second, failure and fault are virtually inseparable in most households, organisations, and cultures. Third, there are three identified areas in which mistakes fall: preventable, complexity-related, and intelligent.

Every child learns at some point that admitting failure means taking the blame. That is why in coaching leaders, individuals, and teams, there is an understanding that so few organisations have shifted to a culture of psychological safety, in which the rewards of learning from failure can be fully realized (Harvard Business Review, 2011). Therefore, if you are not careful, a culture of blame can develop, which can stifle creativity and innovation within your organisation. The table below shows 50% no improvement, and 20–30 percent of the projects failed.

Table IResearch data

Type of change	Successful (%)	Degree of success Neutral (%)	Failed (%)
Total quality management (TQM)	29	50	21
Revitalization	16	50	34
Vision, values, attitudes	32	–	–
Business process systems (BPS)	27	–	–
Information technology	20	–	–

Source: Carr (1995)

CEOs Reed Hastings, Jeff Bezos, and James Quensey all confirm there is no learning without failing. Likewise, there is no success without setbacks. The business world is operating in markets with volatility, uncertainty, complexity, and ambiguity. Encourage workers to be open about failings. Trials in projects should be the basis of innovation as this approach eradicates fear.

In researching an article in the HBR notes, if a team member on a Toyota assembly line spots a problem, or even a potential problem, they are encouraged to pull a rope called the cord, which immediately initiates a diagnostic and problem-solving process. Production continues unimpeded if the problem can be remedied in less than a minute. Otherwise, production is halted—despite the loss of revenue entailed—until the failure is understood and resolved. How has this been possible?

Jeffrey Liker highlights, "Toyota cultivates an inspiring and challenging work environment. Their ongoing strategy is for new "lean leaders" to grow continuously. The company offers on-the-job coaching of its leaders during their whole career, by sensei or experienced mentors to unceasingly deepen and broaden their management skills.

Acting as a sensei involves improving processes and people simultaneously. Do not force people to implement a solution. Instead, coach, encourage, and challenge them to improve their work, problem-solving, and leadership skills. Align local improvement efforts horizontally and vertically, ensuring higher goals are accomplished, such as an increased flow end to end, while also having everyone contribute to the company's mission.

Fred Fiedler presented his leadership contingency model theory, which proposes that effective employee performance depends upon the quality of leadership and coaching, not just the competency of employees. A leader's ability is contingent upon situational factors that tap into their capabilities, preferred leadership style, and behaviour. This theory propounded that those leaders should adopt the style that best suits the situation and immediately stimulates employee performance. An effective leader has a responsibility to provide guidance and share the knowledge to the employee, to lead them for better performance and make them an expert in maintaining the quality. To become the head of all the team members is such a great responsibility. The introduction of clear standards of leadership promotes the core values and maturity of their role and responsibility. As the situation affects which functions the leaders carry out, it would also affect how the functions are performed.

Left to our own devices, most of us will speed through or avoid failure analysis altogether. Another reason is that analysing organisational failures requires inquiry, openness, patience, and tolerance for causal ambiguity. Yet managers typically admire and are rewarded for decisiveness, efficiency, and action—not thoughtful reflection. That is why the right culture is so influential.

A survey of 506 CEOs from around the world, conducted in 2000 and published in 2001 by the Conference Board and Accenture, shows some of the major market challenges today (see below).

Changes in type/level of competition	40.7%
Impact of the internet	38.3%
Industry consolidation	37.4%
Downward pressure on prices	33.4%
Shortage of key skills	31.6%
Changing technology	21.9%
Changes in supply/distribution systems	19.2%
Access to/cost of capital	16.6%
Regulatory issues (labour, market access, etc.)	15.0%
Currency issues	7.7%

(Deutsch, 1949; Johnson and Johnson, 2000) There is clear evidence that shows that goals that are competitive or individualistic should be avoided if teamwork is desired. Groups can be structured so that they will co-operate, compete, or act individualistically.

A company like LEGO re-invests realised profitability and encourages exploration of various ideas, and these no doubt either succeed or fail. The company has now ventured into movies, which have been a success, and this inspiration to explore alternative options fosters creativity and evinces the company's willingness to adapt to change. The founding member of LEGO failed twice before the business became a success. LEGO uses the mantra, "Watch what works and follow where your customers lead you" (www.theleader shipnetwork.com). A talented carpenter, who went through financial difficulties, made all his workers redundant. He lost his wife but did not give up the responsibility of his four children. He made wooden toys for his boys, and they enjoyed the toys, which gave him a business idea. The video referenced below is informative about creativity, and makes for interesting viewing.

https://www.youtube.com/watch?v=qr_dTySMl7s

For example, with the invention of artificial intelligence (IA), creativity for change is of utmost importance. Senior management in organisations need to strategically motivate employees to perform and align themselves to the impending changes AI will bring. This may require making mistakes in the process, or building creative marketing strategies to drive the retention of satisfied customers, whose needs are accurately met with the assurance of their privacy being maintained.

For example, the Agile Project Management (diagram below) or Prince 2 tools can help companies have a forum of trial and error, to propel product research and design in a safe environment where blame is minimised.

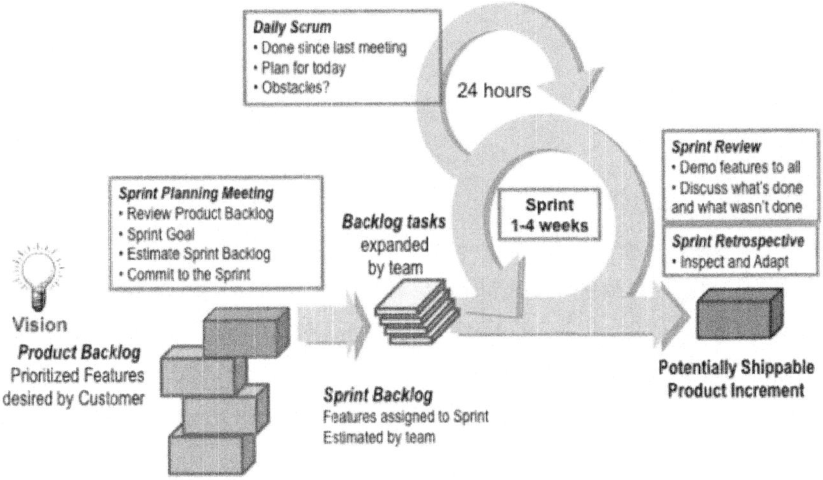

Source: www.googlescholar.com

The Schon (1984) model of reflection can be a useful tool to help teams reflect on their actions and designs, to review what went well and what needs improving. Allowing storytelling provides an environment for transforming a company and employee/team engagement to construct creative project development. The other benefit is consultation and customer feedback during the design process, to ensure that the product meets customer requirements and needs.

Failure indeed inspires creativity. Several issues confronted Amazon's design team when customer feedback revealed that their voice-assisted technology device laughed at inappropriate times and was deemed too scary. This major technological development was not quite right in the beginning. The team went back to the drawing board. Would that be considered a failure? In finding a solution for these problems, the teams involved will undoubtedly be inspired to find a solution creatively. Amazon strategic leaders need to continue fostering a non-blaming culture as they spearhead and venture into new technological developments (www.wired.co.uk).

In career leadership coaching, it is important to understand that influential, dynamic, and collaborative strategic leadership holds the keys to fostering effective teamwork. It utilises motivating, coaching, and inspiring creative work environments, where failure is viewed as an opportunity to improve research design and product development.

In coaching leaders and teams, it has to be acknowledged that managing teams means managing differing individual characteristics. Your diverse team members have different backgrounds, including ages, cultures, genders, races, and classes. Yet all individual employees require management acknowledgment, global encouragement, and meaningful contributions, without blaming, by viewing failings as opportunities to learn. This management approach encourages genuine observance of knowledgeable and respected strategic leadership experts.

Through strategic leadership and collaboration with HR, accounting, IT, marketing, design, and research, all employees feel they are involved in the company's drive to promote adaptation, change, and creativity. To meet the current climate of technological developments that are sweeping businesses, your leadership style needs to adapt to change and creativity.

During the COVID-19 lockdown, entrepreneurial leaders and a lot of aspiring entrepreneurs connected on Clubhouse, which is an iPhone-only, voice-chatting app where individuals can host and join different conversations. Upon opening the app, you are met with a list of "rooms" that you can join, or you can create your own room. Each room has a different topic. Coaching and mentoring ideas were and continue to be discussed, often hosted by an expert or pioneer in the field, and ideas are shared to inspire and encourage. Plugging into such platforms can be an eye opener, and confirms how disruptive technologies are changing the national and global organisations.

Master Key 6

Time Management, Self-Control, and Trusting Others

With that in mind, the 6th Master Key is focused on attributes that contribute to positive relationships, both personally and professionally. The first aspect of this key is time management and how it can contribute to your financial freedom.

Time Management Leads to Financial Freedom

"Life is not just the passing of time. Life is the collection of experiences and their intensity."
– Jim Rohn

Make it your requirement to take charge of your time, your health, and your financial wall, and impose it on yourself to self-develop.

All of us have the same 24 hours in a day. As leaders, we are in the unique position to prioritise how we spend that time. When we employ time management skills, then we put ourselves in the position to maximize our productivity. The goal is to make the most of all the time you are given. That does not mean just being busy and filling hours with various tasks that have no purpose. The ants are busy, but that does not mean they are accomplishing anything.

The key is not to just spend time doing something, but to invest your time, just as you would your money. To get the best return on that investment, you need to strategise how you use your time every day. Review this. Earlier, I talked about the importance of choosing and incorporating habits that help you to reach your goals. Review these. When it comes to managing your time effectively, habits can be key to getting the most out of your time or squandering it.

When I was undertaking my first degree in international business and economics, I was a single mother trying to balance the workload of a full-time degree, plus a part-time job to help sustain my family during this time. I had been fortunate enough to get a day job at Kingfisher plc, on the training and development team, during the two days a week that I was not at university. Working on this team, which was part of the Kingfisher fast-track development scheme training department, I got my first taste of mentoring and coaching. That experience whet my appetite and inspired me to continue down this path that would help others to discover the leader they are within.

You might be wondering what work this department was doing that sparked my interest so completely. They were targeting the top 5 to 10 universities in the UK, with the goal of attracting future leaders to the organisation. We had a list of criteria and attributes that they were looking for in these future leaders, including time management.

Back then, time management was seen as a highly prized attribute. In today's professional landscape, leaders need to prioritise how they spend their time. It cannot be overemphasised. The challenge is how to manage the time wasters that are found everywhere, including the devices we all carry with us every day. Yes, I am talking about your phone. It is important to make it a habit to have an agenda before you make phone/Zoom or Microsoft Teams platforms. Internet use and social media can end up sucking away hours of our day, simply with the endless scrolling. Discipline is important. While there are business and professional benefits for those who use the various social media platforms, leaders need to be balanced. That can even include setting time limits for social media, not only for yourself but for those on your team.

Time can speed by so quickly, leaving you with unfulfilled dreams and goals. If you do not manage your time well, then it is lost to you. That being said, how you decide to use your time can reflect the lifestyle that you want to live. For instance, as an entrepreneur, you might want the flexibility to travel and explore. By opting to invest in properties, the high frequency Forex, and investment trading, you can create a stream of income that allows you to live the way you want, by giving you financial freedom. That financial freedom gives you the ability to assist those in your community in a meaningful way, using your time to impact those less fortunate than yourself.

Personally, I have made a commitment to be involved in work that involves vulnerable children, such as those who might have experienced sexual abuse, were abandoned, or have been neglected by their parents due to drug use, substance misuse, or domestic violence. In each of these instances, a child was left behind to pick up the pieces from that trauma, and I believe in leading within my community to address these traumas and to do what I can to help them in the healing process, as a school governor being involved in supporting the success of a school. Children deserve the best chance to be supported and to learn in a neutral learning environment, with teachers who understand and identify their strengths so that they can thrive and succeed.

Our goals and dreams might be different, but in the end, not managing our time well can end up being an obstacle that stops us from leading and contributing to our communities, locally, nationally, and internationally, in an effective and meaningful way. Often, our careers can make us think we can do only one thing at a time, when the reality is that through investing and strategic choices that lead to financial freedom, you give yourself the ability to earn a living while focusing on your purpose and what brings you joy.

Right now, I want you to list all the things that you would like to do if you had financial freedom. Then you need to make a list of the time wasters that are creeping into your day. Recognise that those time wasters and bad habits are impeding your ability to achieve financial freedom. Lead by example, and eliminate time wasters. Doing so can help you to shape the future you want, instead of a future filled with regrets.

Building Trust by Delegation

In every home around the world, parents have a number of tasks to complete each day so that the members of the family are clean, fed, and sheltered. However, no parent ever completes all these tasks alone. They often choose to delegate tasks to each other and their children. The result is that they can get all the tasks accomplished and meet everyone's needs daily.

Maslow's hierarchy of needs, a motivational theory outlining five categories of human behaviour, which include psychological, starting at the bottom, and then safety, love, belonging, esteem, and self-actualisation, reaching one's full potential, at the very top. Responsible caregivers and parents strive to balance when providing for children.

In the professional world, leaders and their teams operate on a basis of delegation. The leader analyzes the team and identifies strengths and weaknesses, and then delegates tasks accordingly. That leader assumes those tasks will be completed correctly, because he trusts those on his team. Delegation is, at its core, a form of trust building. When you lead your team and show them that you trust in their abilities, they are willing to do more, and the productivity of the team is elevated. Knowing what motivates them is important for each individual, the team, and the organisation.

At the same time, you have to be approachable. After all, mistakes are going to be made. A learning curve is inevitable, but that does not mean you cannot have expectations. Still, by empowering those on your team, you give your team members a chance to tap into their inner leader.

When I was contracted to work for the internationally renowned Taylor Wessing solicitors, on their training and development team, I was fascinated by the induction programme of solicitors from top universities, including top intellectual property solicitors. When they joined the organisation, the first days of the induction programme entailed a tailored, structured programme to allow each employee to learn the company's systems and processes at their own pace. This system empowered the employees, motivating them. They were not afraid to make mistakes. Such a coaching approach is beneficial for all stakeholders because it reduces intimidation and peer pressure.

My fiancée and I were impressed by an increasing number of employees of a local building contracting company, The Whitelock Group, who meet early each morning before their working day, for a sea swim, originally as a way to keep fit, but this has also enabled them to form a very strong working relationship with co-workers, to the benefit of themselves and the company. This is inspiring.

What type of environment are you creating for your team? Do you give them room to learn and grow? Is there latitude to analyze failures, allowing for improvement of the whole process? Do you sit down with your team members regularly? With the COVID-19 lockdown, do you have virtual Microsoft Teams or Zoom calls, exploring what they are doing now, and areas where they can grow? Do you focus solely on improving weaknesses, or do you acknowledge the strengths and give them tools to get even better?

I ask all these questions because when you lead, you drive the productivity of the team by how you interact with them. The culture you create is based on whether they feel comfortable reaching out to you for guidance and direction. Many mistakes can be made, simply because they feared failing, and your response to that failure.

Perhaps you worked for a boss that constantly criticised your work, questioned your competency, and ended up leaving you feeling degraded. That type of leadership does not result in a productive team or individuals who are excited to create and innovate. I encourage you to look at how you are approaching your team, and the environment being produced as a result. If it has become toxic, then you will not get their best. They will move on to leaders who value what they contribute, and excel with them.

Another aspect of delegation and trust building involves how you spend your time. If you are constantly micromanaging others on your team, then you are limiting your own productivity. Consider delegation as a way to increase the number of things being accomplished, without you having to necessarily touch every aspect of the process.

When I have coaching conversations with leaders and other coaches, the issue of delegation always comes up. It is so relevant because you cannot physically do everything. Delegation is your chance to develop trust in others, and recognise that your high standards can be met by those on your team. Overseeing a process does not mean watching every detail be accomplished, but means training others to take over and accomplish the detail work.

Coaching and mentoring others to develop the skills needed to complete a task and to be accountable for their actions, is a sign of a great leader. Avoid the mindset (Mindset Of Excellence: Think and Grow Rich and Believe In Yourself) that people cannot do the job as best as you can. Individual team members have their own areas of expertise and strengths, so trust them to perform accordingly. You have your own strengths, so use them to inspire others to maximize their strengths.

I encourage you to delegate certain tasks to team members. This frees up time to focus on higher-value activities, as you are a visionary, and to make effective use of your time to be more productive. Delegation gives you, as a leader and coach, time for strategic thinking, and more time to concentrate on those tasks that only you can perform, such as leading and coaching your teams to their next level.

One of the best coaches of the century was Bill Campbell. He taught that many of the other skills of management can be delegated, but not coaching. The path to success in a fast-moving, highly competitive, technology-driven business world is to form high-performing teams and give them the resources and freedom to do great things. An essential component of high-performing teams is a leader who is both a savvy manager and a caring coach. At this, Bill Campbell was the best there ever was (Schmidt and Rosenberg et al). When I talk about leadership, I believe it starts with understanding the importance of modelling what you want from your team. There should not be a double standard. Instead of thinking that you know it all, embrace the benefits of coaching and mentoring as part of your self-development, thus inspiring your team to do the same. With that in mind, how can companies and organisations incorporate self-development as part of their strategic growth plan?

Keep Learning to Increase Your Self-Development

Based on all the experience I have gained over 20 years, I am now a certified Gallup strengths coach. I help those I coach/train or supervise, individually and as teams, using the Gallup Strengths Finder Assessment tool, which identifies your strengths and talents.

As a coach, I am also a member of the International Coaching Federation (ICF), and this helps me be aware of other coaching tools that help me to determine the best steps to take with those working with me. One such tool is the GROW model, which is an acronym for Goal, Reality, Options, and Will. We start by defining their goals, determining where they are now (reality), the options available to achieve their goals, and then helping to motivate them to go after those goals (will). Think about your team for a moment. There are likely many things they wish to accomplish using defined goals. I often find it necessary to dig deeper, to understand why the goals they have identified remain incomplete. Most of the time, either the will or the knowledge is simply unavailable. My job is to identify the missing pieces and help them to fill in those necessary pieces.

The client or team member will have their own identified goal. They can have a goal for that individual session, and a larger goal for the over-arching process of working with you as a coach or mentor. I incorporate the Motivational Interviewing model when I am curious about a client's thought process, particularly how they perceive certain behaviours, such as imposter syndrome or low self-confidence. It helps clients to explore and resolve their ambivalence. That process helps them to find the best solution within their strengths. It is a non-biased, non-oppressive, non-judgmental, non-confrontational, and non-adversarial option to help someone develop their strengths and self-confidence even further.

When working with entrepreneurs and leaders in the social work field, or working with vulnerable children, adults, and families, it helps the client identify their intrinsic values and the goals that align with those, and then to align their behaviours to achieve those goals. I also use tools from my psychotherapy training and counselling. The coaching process throughout this time involves proactive active listening and a non-judgmental approach.

With today's politically correct world, it can be difficult for leaders to not be afraid to challenge poor performance, hold employees accountable for the failure to meet deadlines, or to align with organisational aims and objectives. Professional boundaries are fundamentally important. This can be a sensitive issue. This could happen when an individual is being over familiar. Where is that elusive boundary? Never put up with people who cross ethical lines: lying, bullying, or harassing or mistreating colleagues. The harder cases are the ones where the person doesn't cross these lines. How do you determine when the damage a person causes exceeds their considerable contributions? There is no perfect answer to this, but there are a few warning signs. All of these are coachable, but if there is no change, they shouldn't be tolerated. You as a leader need to be fair and provide platforms for negotiations and discussion to encourage inclusion and participation.

The Key Performance Indicator requires a clear plan, dates, and specific actions to meet the business's objectives, return on investment, and customer needs. It can be a way to connect with your employees and team, holding them accountable while keeping them involved in the process of defining what they are taking on. It is vital, in this current business landscape, that companies factor coaching and accessing external training into their budgets, such as the services of an accredited Gallup strengths coach.

A Howard research covered 1000 employees, asking how often they have seen senior leaders challenge the status quo or ask employees across industries nationwide to think outside the box. The answers demonstrated that leadership truly models what they want from their teams:

- 42% said they never or almost never.
- 32% said sometimes.
- 26% said fairly often or very often.
- Only 3% said always.

Notice that organisations talk constantly about creativity and innovation, but research suggests that they are doing the exact opposite in how they lead behind closed doors. With that in mind, here are some questions that are meant to get at the heart of how you are developing your team, and how your leadership might be contributing or blocking that progress.

- What's going well for you and your team this week?
- How are you feeling at work lately?
- What's the best thing that happened to you this week, either at work or outside of it?
- If you owned the company, what's one thing you would do differently?
- What were some great contributions made by other team members recently? How did you recognise those contributions?
- How are you supporting or providing opportunities for self-development for your team?

I have personally spent thousands of pounds attending self-development courses. My MBA was completed, and I had become a mindfulness and well-being practitioner, a neuro-linguistic programming practitioner, and a master with Richard Bandler added to this, along with psychotherapy training in search of understanding the human mind and behaviour. There were also setbacks, such as losing thousands to a local British Forex trading company. These things happen, and self-development is often about finding ways to address disappointments and setbacks effectively.

I have learnt a lot from these experiences. I put it down to making an effort to find a way to avoid making those mistakes again. Thankfully, I came across IM Academy, an American-based trading platform founded by Christopher Terry, which teaches all the basics of Forex trading, with clear modules to follow, for individuals like you and me. I have found it very informative and beneficial as they have more than 150 educators to learn from. I liken it to an open university of Forex trading. In an effort to research how young people can learn financial freedom, I came across an article about the youngest Forex trader. He is South African and is a young Forex millionaire. And there are also other traders and investors younger than 30 years, who made million-dollar fortunes in their twenties (e.g., Shezi, born 1993, reported in 2016, aged 23). These skills can be learned, and learning from a responsible company is key as you are taught about risk to reward ratio, and never to overtrade.

Now, when I recommend different learning opportunities to others, I occasionally come across the argument that certain things are "pyramid schemes" that are flawed and meant to suck resources from individuals. In my opinion, everything is a pyramid scheme, from the military to business. You have one person on top, and everyone is below them. We recommend products that we like to family and friends without getting paid for it. Therefore, I believe it is important to understand that those recommendations are based on how those products or services were being relevant to you, and where you are in your self-development.

Seeking self-development for whatever reason, and depending on your strengths, is something relevant to you. Others may not see it that way, but you decide what is good for you and those you coach. All my adult life, I have been involved in helping people, wherever I have been, to focus on the positive aspects of themselves. As an accredited strengths coach, I focus on helping clients with strengths assessment tools, to know them, claim them, and apply them to every aspect of their day-to-day activities, to lead successfully in a professional environment.

For free sheets on time management, log on to www.coachingtoday.com.

For a free gift of a recommended list of self-help books, visit www.careerleadershipcoachingtoday.com.

Now let's shift to discussing how you can lead with compassion and accountability, while investing in yourself as a leader during these unprecedented times.

Reflection Notes

Master Key 7

Lead With Self-Compassion and Accountability

7

This period of time during the pandemic has been challenging for everyone. As I have heard often, we might all be in the same storm, but not everyone is in the same boat. The standards of the perfect family and perfect life have been upended as we are all dealing with being at home and isolated from our social support systems. In many ways, there is a level of compassion that is necessary, both for ourselves and for others.

Self-compassion is really no different from the compassion that we have for others. One of the essential aspects of compassion is recognising the suffering of others and being moved to care about their situation, and having a desire to help them in some way to alleviate that suffering. It also means that you are willing to offer kindness and understanding when someone makes mistakes or fails, instead of judging them harshly. Fundamentally, compassion helps you to recognise that suffering, failure, and imperfection as part of our shared human experience. Love your neighbour as you love yourself, and forgive those that trespass against you.

Self-compassion taps into the same emotional and mental response that you have for someone else, but now you have compassion for yourself. Instead of having a stiff upper lip mentality, you acknowledge how difficult it is in the moment, and focus on giving yourself comfort and care so that you can get back up.

In line with that, self-compassion involves several important aspects. The first is self-kindness versus self-judgment. Social media often has us comparing ourselves constantly to an unachievable standard, making us critical of our choices and leadership, both personally and professionally. People cannot always be or get everything exactly as they would wish for it to be. Self-criticism can negatively impact your mental and emotional health, making you question your leadership strengths.

Humility can be a way to counteract that self-criticism, recognising that mistakes can be made, and that you can learn from them. It also helps you to recognise the contributions of others and how important they can be to helping your productivity and leadership.

One of my local vicars sent out a newsletter during the COVID-19 lockdown. There was a quote included by Mahatma Gandhi, which said, "When I despair, I remember that all through history, the way of truth and love has always won."

There have always been murderers and tyrants, those who foster injustice and introduce negativity into the environment. For a time, they may seem to be invincible, but in the end, they always fail. Compassion and connection are critical in this process. The newsletter further shared, "It can be easy for us to focus on all the bad news, which is what the media gives us, spreading gloom and doom. We cannot spend all our time worrying nor praying about it. We need to focus on the God who cares more for this world than we ever can, who gave himself in Jesus to restore it to harmony."

When I reflected on this, I realised the importance of self-compassion through what we allow ourselves to experience. Giving ourselves permission, and making choices about what we listen to and what we watch in our homes, can have a profound effect on our well-being and mental health. These unprecedented times have called for places of worship to adjust to suit the changing climate. It is definitely not just business as usual. To meet the needs of the congregation, services have been delivered over video streaming services via Microsoft Teams, Zoom, Skype, Facebook/YouTube Live, and related social media platforms. Who would have ever thought this would happen? Disruptive times require leaders to come up with solutions to fit those disruptive times, being flexible and supporting innovative processes.

As a leader in these disruptive times, you hold responsibility to steer the ship of your organisation, remaining calm and reassured. Wearing my social work hat, I was reflecting on the times I was involved in management roles, where I was supervising and supporting, mentoring, and coaching newly qualified social workers. Intuition and emotional intelligence play a part when assessing and dealing with the complex assessment to safeguard vulnerable children and families. The capacity to be aware of, control, and express one's emotions, and to handle interpersonal relationships judiciously and empathetically, is key.

For example, when I was doing supervision, reminding those I supervised and coached to be in the moment and to be present with a focused aim, and not be wrong footed by other issues or adults, it called for intense awareness and accountability of complex tasks. This was especially when working with and safeguarding vulnerable children and adults, where there were issues of mental health, sexual abuse, neglect, modern day slavery, child sexual exploitation, domestic violence, drugs and alcohol misuse, child trafficking, and gangs. Coaching and mentoring in this field can be intense. It is of paramount importance during reflective sessions and career development appraisals to factor in accountability and self-compassion. Aligning with this effort is the essential tool of mindfulness. You can exercise mindfulness anytime to keep yourself calm, especially when the situation appears to be escalating. For example, here is a mindfulness tool you can use in a variety of situations. Note that it takes just a few seconds, but it can really help you to de-escalate your emotional response.

ABC Awareness of Breath Mindfulness Practice:

A is Acknowledge
B is Breath
C is Connection

This quick exercise can ground you during a stressful or demanding situation. Start by breathing in and counting 1, 2, 3; then breathe out and count 1, 2, 3. Give yourself time so that you do not rush and speak before you are prepared to.

As you take in that initial breath, feel where the sensations of breathing are most detectable. Feel the air passing through your nostrils, where sensations of breathing are most detectable. You might also note the way your navel area rises and falls during your breathing exercise. Place your attention on the nostril or naval area, depending on where you feel the sensations of breathing the most. Now remain aware of the sensations of breathing in and out at your chosen area of attention.

Breathing in, you are aware you are breathing in. Breathing out, you are aware you are breathing out. Let your breathing be natural; observe your natural breath, coming in and going out, at either the nostrils or naval area. Do not try to alter your breath. If you unconsciously start to alter your breath, be aware that you are doing so, relax, and allow the breath to return to its natural rhythm.

When I worked for multinational companies, including Cable and Wireless, the director, Ann Sullivan, was my coach and mentor in the global mobile department, which had a budget exceeding multimillion-pound projects. She always showed compassion, and genuinely listened to what team members contributed. If anything went wrong during a project, she did not blame others but acknowledged where the breakdowns occurred. As a leader, she always stated that setting up projects required clearly defined plans to allow monitoring and tracking. With that in mind, let's talk about what you need to successfully move a project forward.

Attention to Detail for Successful Leadership

One of the things I noted about the most successful leaders is that they were clear about their expectations and the parameters of any project they had their team tackle. When a project was successful, they benefitted from the attention to detail early in the process. Here are five attributes that are continually and consistently followed by leaders who successfully achieve their team goals:

- Meticulously defining the project
- Engaging the project team
- Preparing project plan(s)
- Defining your project control
- Engaging your stakeholders

Having a project checklist always helps leaders to enable solution-based coaching and mentoring. Specifically stating the business drivers, scope, and objectives for projects (i.e. why we are doing it, what you will produce, when you will produce it, how you will approach the project, and who will be involved), can often be essential to engaging your team and maximising their productivity. This process also allows for clarity and ownership of tasks, thus opening channels for accountability, monitoring, and tracking. If there are gaps, leadership needs to challenge the team to be innovative, to address the gaps with clear processes, not blaming but challenging them for improvement.

Talking of change, the US Environmental Protection Agency (EPA) announced that all paperback book production will stop in 2030, due to the damaging impact of deforestation. All books from 2030 will be in digital form (electronic, audio) only. Over the last decade, I've seen a BIG shift from what seemed the traditional way of doing things. Now, more than 50% of my readership listen to my books on Audible. People are busier and more distracted than ever, so audiobook and podcast listening has replaced sitting down and reading a book anyway.

Do you think this is an important step in our technological and environmental evolution, or the death of one of our greatest institutions? Take time to think and reflect on this change. As a leader and a coach, consider any changes your own organisation can make to plan for future projects in relation to the impact of this shift.

That being said, these days, attention to detail can seem difficult to achieve. Let's talk about what that means for leaders, and how investing in yourself can be an essential part of leading during these unprecedented times.

Shifting Times Require an Investment in You

The uncertain times we are living in pose a great challenge. What used to be the norm is no longer. There is a lot that is unknown. This can be a scary place for everyone, even more so for the leaders that people look up to for answers. We know from research that living with uncertainty may be more challenging than coping with a known catastrophe. It is difficult to plan and be strategic. The pace of change is also very fast. This can be overwhelming. Many circumstances now facing organisation leaders are unprecedented, without reference points or previous experience to draw upon.

Leaders and managers have courage, and they face pressure to continue performing their roles, perhaps not knowing how their usual leadership skills and styles fit with the new circumstances. How do they stay in touch with, motivate, and support their workforce? How do they decide which staff to furlough, when and how to do it, when and how to bring them back, and how does being furloughed impact individual team members and the team dynamics?

Human resources (HR) departments may be coordinating furloughs while operating with reduced staff within their own team. Other HR issues cannot be addressed. For organisations that have increased the number of team members working from home, there may be a wide range of concerns, including pressures on staff with young children, structuring the working day and week, as well as establishing new collaborative links between departments. On an individual level, some staff may feel their workload has increased, while others may be feeling underutilised or disconnected. In the private sector, many small and medium enterprises will be battling to keep afloat, and even to avoid closure. Activity is not impact. Just being busy does not equal productivity. Identify activities that are intentional, and use them to stretch towards a greater impact.

Another positive way to improve your life during this challenging time is to read and learn something new every day. I am a believer in learning something new every day.

Something that everyone wants is success. This can be in business, relationships, healthy living, spirituality, and family. For some, it comes naturally, but for others, it is a skill that they have acquired after hard work and effort. Yes, that skill cannot be acquired without investing in yourself and putting in the effort.

I recommend you use self-help books, like *Rich Dad, Poor Dad* and Napoleon Hill's *Think and Grow Rich, The Power of Persuasion.* I have read both a dozen times each. "It's an eternal mantra that men receive more money from their ability to get others to perform than they could possibly earn from their own efforts," is a good mantra of Hill's to adopt.

More than ever, we need to rely on and invest in our self-development and coaching in today's disruptive artificial intelligence and internet world. Knowing and supporting those we coach, to identify and know their strengths and talents, is key to their success in this fast-paced technological world.

Research shows that individuals who experienced negative developmental experiences in childhood may lack social skills and the desire for closeness in adulthood. As a leader and coach, you need to be mindful that the individuals you work with, coach, lead, or mentor are coming from different backgrounds. In the last chapter of this book, I researched and put together childhood stories of some of the great disruptive leaders of our time, to help you glean on how individual disruptive leaders started their businesses and inspired change. These stories include those who dealt with a difficult childhood, adoption, disabilities, and issues of race, age, or gender. Yet despite all their challenges, none of them let those issues stop them or hinder the achievement of their dreams. Therefore, do not be quick to dismiss those who have these challenges in their background, but embrace the strengths that they have as a result of those experiences, including resiliency.

Research shows that at times, traumatic childhood experiences can rob adults of healthy interpersonal relationships and communication skills, as they seek isolation and emotional distance. As a leader and coach seeking to help clients, I have found that using Gallup's *Now, Discover Your Strengths* helps, as it highlights that we are guided by the belief that good is the opposite of bad. For centuries, mankind has pursued its fixation with fault finding and failing. Doctors have studied disease to learn about health. Psychologists have investigated sadness to learn about joy.

Therapists have looked into the causes of divorce to learn about happy marriage. In schools and workplaces around the world, individuals have been encouraged to identify, analyze, and correct their weaknesses to become strong. This advice is well intended but misguided. Faults and failings deserve study, but they reveal little about strengths. Strengths have their own patterns.

To excel in one's chosen field and to find lasting satisfaction in doing so, one needs to understand their unique patterns. Children, students, parents, leaders, teachers, life and sports coaches, teams, and undergraduate and MBA students, need to be supported to become experts at finding, describing, applying, practicing, and refining their strengths and talents. Children are let down if the adults and teachers around them do not focus on motivating, encouraging, and praising them on their strengths and talents, rather than focusing on their weaknesses, and telling the children about how they failed.

When I was in school, I had a teacher who always talked down to me and would not include me in group discussions. I would raise my hand, but she would not pick me to answer, even though my test scores were extremely high. When I was voted to be a head girl, she refused to let me take this position, so I ended up being a prefect and deputy head. I did not understand why she was behaving that way.

Why am I sharing this? Simply put, a teacher plays a significant role in a child's life. I now make it a point that when I speak to teachers and head teachers in schools, I remind them about the fundamentally pivotal role they hold, to shape and influence their students' lives. When I spoke with different individuals, they remembered teachers who helped them or those who made them hate school. I encourage the teachers reading this book to remember that you can make or break a child's dreams. So be mindful of the fact that in your class, there are future leaders who need your encouragement and motivation. Spot their strengths and talents. They are the disruptive leaders and change makers of tomorrow.

As a leader, you can have a similar impact on your team. Show an interest in people's lives. Engage in small talk and be genuine when you ask about their family or friends. Be sensitive to those individuals that do not have families. Being sincere can reap powerful benefits, including earning trust and respect from the individuals on your team. There was a 2010 study that concluded that having these sorts of substantive conversations, as opposed to just meaningless small talk, makes people happier because they feel valued.

A lack of success in projects throughout organisations is often due to objectives not being clear, not enough communication, senior management not supporting projects, inadequate scheduling, and the failure to put together and choose brilliant ideas. This results from leaders and employees not understanding the unique strengths and talents of those on their teams. Just putting a project team together, without considering or understanding the team members' strengths, can reduce the profitability and productivity of the team, and minimise the organisation's return on investment. By putting aside your focus on their weaknesses, and exploring their intricate strengths through the Clifton Strengths assessment tool, you can discover the key domain themes of your team's strengths, and maximize their potential. Self-development as a leader and a team is a continuous process; therefore, keep learning. Take time to relax, reflect, and meditate, so you can bring responsible management into play.

Your People Make You a Leader

Coaching during the COVID-19 lockdown and beyond requires you to understand that your people make you a leader. Breathe your strengths and power into your team. Affirm their strengths as you benefit from your own. Your mindset (Mindset Of Excellence: Think and Grow Rich and Believe In Yourself) should focus on believing in yourself, walking with the belief that all things are possible if you believe and follow up that belief with actions. Faith without works is dead, and the same applies to belief without action. No one said you might not fail. Pick yourself up and keep going. As a leader, you are predestined for great things.

For a free sheet of these transactional leadership tools, log on to www.careerleadershipcoachingtoday.com.

Now let's dive into how you can lead more fully during these disruptive times that are driving change in multiple industries and communities around the globe.

Master Key 8

Lead with Confidence in Disruptive Business, Global AI, and Pandemic Landscapes

8

The unprecedented times we are experiencing highlight the challenges for leaders around the world. Universities have faced the challenge to educate employable and entrepreneurial graduates in the wake of a rapidly changing world. The economic and business landscape is being rewritten by agile, disruptive technologies. Artificial intelligence, climate change, and pandemics are the order of the day, which means leaders need to adapt quickly, and encourage creativity and innovation throughout their organisations in order for them to not just survive but to thrive.

"The path to success is to
take massive, determined action."
– Tony Robbins

Businesses need to establish new ways of working. Coaches need to establish new ways to deliver services that are beneficial, and which add value to organisations and the individuals they coach. If we consider the family home as a business unit, children are tomorrow's leaders; therefore, parents (as leaders) need to establish new ways of parenting as children spend more time on devices, as well as face issues relating to identity, mental health, peer pressure, self-harming, isolation, and a lack of understanding how to communicate effectively with their children.

As highlighted in previous chapters, my mother has played a pivotal role in my life, as well as being a source of strength throughout my childhood and adult life. It is through her hard work that I can enjoy the blessings of the Lord and the fruits of my labour today. I honour my mother, who is now in her 70s. With the Zimbabwe heritage, she always encouraged me to get an education, saying this would open my mind, and doors of opportunities. While she might have employed an old-school approach, her advice was always motivational. Today, she remains one of my primary cheerleaders, encouraging me to keep reaching beyond and exploring other opportunities. I have spoken to many people during my coaching journey, and most people who talk about bringing up their children, say that no one taught them how to parent; however, what is apparent is the need for parents to be confident in making firm, parental decisions, and giving direction, routines, and boundaries, allowing children to be children. Children learn from this.

My mother acknowledges Father Arthur ShearlyCripps, who worked closely with her father (my maternal grandfather), whom I never met, as he passed away before I was born. There is a book called 'The Dust Diaries' by Woen Sheers about my mother says, every time I enter any meeting, travel, or talk on any platform, that I am a result of both my maternal and paternal grandparents, my father, and her input. Together, all of them contributed to where my siblings and I are today, and to all we have accomplished. They gave us wisdom and inspiration, and also encouraged us during the difficult times. The truth is that every one of us is a product of history and, as individuals, decide for ourselves which direction and path to take in relation to business/jobs and family life. Each of us is making our own history in different ways. Whatever you are doing, be encouraged by what you have already accomplished, and by whatever your genealogy is of those who have accomplished before you. My psychotherapy and social work training taught me that secure attachments between parents and children are the foundation for optimal development. Therefore, it is of high importance to encourage parents to deal with their own issues, if not for themselves, for the sake of their children. If parents are not able to do this, their children may do all right in life if they find other people who substitute for emotionally available parents, but they would do much better if their parents had attended to their own resolved issues. I drew strength in knowing that if parents fail us, there are other adults or caregivers who are able to love and nurture us by God's amazing grace.

When I look at the issue of parenting, in my opinion, we are all foster children: either fostered by our parents or by other caregivers (in their absence, for whatever reason). No matter what your background, you should not dwell on the past; make your world the way you want it. You can make it; you have the power within you to change the course of your life, no matter what challenges you may face, whether it's the loss of a business, a job, or a loved one, a relationship breakdown, or facing health issues.

There is a saying: "Time heals." For everything, there is a season; a time for every activity under heaven. A time to be born and a time to die, a time to plant and a time to plant, and a time to harvest. Our lives contain a mixture of joy and sorrow, pleasure and pain, harmony and struggle. Each season has its appropriate time in the cycle of life. Nothing stays the same, and we, as God's children, must learn to accept and adjust to life.

Leading and coaching during the COVID-19 disruption has presented challenges for us all. Knowing ourselves, our strengths, and digging deep in our conscious and subconscious minds to keep a positive mindset (Mindset Of Excellence: Think and Grow Rich and Believe In Yourself) has been key.

Even in education, it is apparent that universities need to prepare the students they educate to meet the demands of the agile work environments. Traditional jobs and career trajectories no longer exist. Historically, people had "jobs for life," but this is no longer the case. The business and job landscape has drastically changed. Ensuring we have the workforce and talents to meet the needs of the rapidly changing business landscape and future, requires a major evolution in how we think about individuals. No longer should it be about their weaknesses, but it should revolve around their strengths.

For instance, powerful forces are reshaping the banking industry. Customer expectations, technological capabilities, regulatory requirements, demographics, and economics are coming together, thus creating an imperative for these organisations to change. Banks need to get ahead of these challenges and retool to win in the next era. They need to execute on today's imperatives, but also radically innovate and transform themselves for whatever the future holds. Note that every one of those powerful forces is at work in other industries around the world. No industry or organisation is immune to the impact of these seismic global shifts.

The changing face of the UK economy, and the world over, for high-street retail shops, is the death of an era. The business world requires graduates and leaders who are clear on their strengths, skills, and talents to remain competitive within their industries. For example, the research firm Forrester estimates that e-commerce is now approaching $200 billion in revenue in the United States alone, and accounts for 9% of total retail sales, up from 5% five years ago. The traditional retail store, with its limited hours and high overhead, is being overturned by the internet, which is open 24/7 throughout the year. Companies like Amazon, that focus on e-commerce, cloud computing, digital streaming, and artificial intelligence, are leading globally. Amazon is one of the Big Five companies in the United States information technology industry, along with Google, Apple, Microsoft, and Facebook; and the likes of traditional companies, like M&S, Next, and House of Frazer, have experienced a downturn. As you know, people can now shop anytime and get almost anything delivered to their doorstep. To be competitive, these businesses must radically rethink how they do business, by shifting resources away from brick-and-mortar locations, to landing pages and customer-friendly websites.

Taking into consideration research that shows a corresponding e-commerce figure is about 10% in the United Kingdom, 3% in Asia-Pacific, and 2% in Latin America, the driving change of the internet is clear. Globally, digital retailing is probably headed towards 15% to 20% of total sales, though the proportion will vary significantly by sector. Moreover, much digital retailing is now highly profitable. Amazon's five-year average return on investment, for example, is 17%, whereas traditional discount and department stores average 6.5% (Harvard Business Review). Strengths-based performance and leadership embrace creativity, flexibility, and adopting change (Clifton and Hodge).

Coaching and mentoring play a fundamental part in establishing best practices for coaching models meant to help future leaders understand themselves, while developing good communication skills with empathy and inclusiveness. Understanding the importance of prioritising and time management is a critical part of preparing the next generation of disruptive thinkers and leaders, which are being nurtured right now in our schools and universities. The demand for MBA/EMBA graduates with highlighted skills and strengths is apparent.

Since universities and schools around the world are often driven by the profit they generate, it is understandable that they adjust to today's ever-changing, disruptive business environment by delivering the kind of revolutionary preparation for their students that meet the expectations of today's employers. Creatively moving, adjusting, realigning, and implementing, with rapid agility, is par for the course of the professional landscape.

COVID-19 also demonstrated that universities and schools around the world need to have a broad-based implementation of internet-based tools, including video lectures, coaching, mentoring, testing, research materials, and more. Open university was strategically ahead of the game in this aspect, providing courses online. The schools that deliver the best are the ones that will offer their students tangible benefits. There is a need to keep up with the Joneses, by not letting competitive nations, with up-and-coming universities, pass them by. There is a danger that employer feedback could be detrimental to a university's reputation as they try to attract the best students in the future.

Now let's take this situation from the student's point of view. As they graduate, if they lack self-awareness, a competitive advantage based upon a broad knowledge and skills foundation, and an understanding of the disruptive nature of AI and the internet, then those students might find themselves unable to articulate or identify their own strengths and talents. The result is that they can end up in the wrong jobs, unhappy with their professional trajectory, and thus not performing to their maximum potential. There is nothing more demoralising to a person than driving or using public transport to go to a job or business they do not like. With the COVID-19 lockdown, they would be waking up and logging on to a device, going through the same emotions, and not enjoying the job. They would be working from a deficit position, instead of a position of strength. The stressed-out worker will never maximize the productivity of an organisation, and could end up being a detriment throughout their career.

Part of what I do in the world of coaching is help my clients recognise how the world is changing, and then how they can maximize their strengths within this shifting landscape. The focus is not on constantly identifying weaknesses and creating goals to minimise them, but to capitalise on strengths and self-development to make them even stronger.

Think about your last workout in the gym. You did some exercises meant to help strengthen specific muscles, but then you focused on doing exercises that would improve the muscles already made strong by past exercise. The goal of all this work is that you end up stronger overall, and your body reaps the benefits.

In the workforce today, and into the future, it is key to find ways to strengthen yourself as a leader. Whenever you are working with a team, contribute creativity, but be open to delegation. Pay attention to the details when creating the project plan, and then allow your team to execute it with their strengths and abilities. Every master key is based upon the idea that you lead best when you know who you are and what you can offer. Humility is also critical, because it allows you to not have a bruised ego if you need to tap into the strengths and knowledge of others to get the job done.

Knowing and understanding your unique traits, your role and attributes as a leader, and how to interpret the behaviours of others based upon their strengths, can give you the greatest potential for meaningful and sustainable relationships and outcomes, both personally and professionally. Involve all those around you in the process of fully realising the goals of the team and the organisation. Being mindful to remain respectful, not talking down to people, and giving back in a constructive way and not a derogatory way, goes a long way in keeping a motivated team of individuals who feel valued. I once worked with a manager who used to shout instructions at people, disregarding the fact that they were working with qualified, skilled, and knowledgeable individuals. This was very demoralising to team members, who ended up leaving the company. What a loss to the company, which had taken steps and invested in training these individuals.

How can you do that effectively? Good communication is often seen as critical for any leader to be successful. Yet, too often, leaders see good communication as a one-way street, where they give orders and direction, while their team listens and takes notes. The truth is that you are not the repository for all the knowledge in the world. Your team has a lot to offer. Active listening skills can help you to hear what they have to offer. Use breakout sessions to hear from and involve all your team members. During these sessions, talk less and listen more. Encouraging your team to be creative does nothing if you are not willing to hear their ideas. Continued allocation of tasks, without regard of how an employee will manage tasks, can put pressure on workers as they will end up not concentrating or allocating sufficient time to pay attention to detail. Blame also stifles creativity, and is demoralising.

Part of any journey of leadership involves questioning, reflecting, and reviewing what you are doing. It is not about self-criticism but about analysing what you are doing well, and then doing more of that. Along the way, you will identify weaknesses, and perhaps you might choose to work on them, but the goal is to take your strengths and use them to drive your leadership.

Many individuals that I speak with have a perspective that has been shaped by various beliefs and values, which are part of who they are. However, that perspective can end up becoming so narrow that it limits our ability to lead effectively. We get stuck in a rut and are unable to see a situation from a different point of view. Reframing is a way to shift your perspective, thus encouraging change and creativity. How can you reframe a situation? By actively listening to others and getting their perspective. Allow what they have to contribute to inform how you view a situation and how you opt to move forward, or the course you choose to take.

When you believe in everyone's strengths, like my mother did, then you have the ability to use those strengths and talents to reframe a discussion. Creativity and innovation can blossom in a place where strengths are the focus, and weaknesses are acknowledged but do not necessarily take centre stage.

Imagine that a critical presentation for your company is being presented over a video conferencing application. Whom do you choose to make that presentation? Do you choose the person who has a great command of the facts but who completely freezes, or the person who can absorb the facts and is completely comfortable with standing in front of others, fielding questions on the fly?

Leaders look for ways to enable themselves to succeed with their teams, and this involves equipping themselves with tools to succeed, even if those tools are the strengths of others. Do not create a culture of blame, where the solution is to find fault with others and not acknowledge or take accountability for your contribution to the current situation. After all, if you model a blame culture, then that is what you will find everyone on your team doing as well. To create change that fires productivity, you need to encourage accountability and a focus on strengths. That focus on strengths involves taking the opportunity to think about fresh ideas, and giving your team a space to share those ideas without judgment. Sometimes the wildest ideas are often the source of the solution that you need, in order to take your team or organisation to the next level. Unblocking your team means discussing, exploring, trying, and testing new ideas or methods. That is where you find the creativity of your team.

Mindfully reflecting is important for improving your leadership. Keep a journal of your thoughts, feelings, and the areas where you showcased excellence, either as part of your team or as a leader. The point is to re-enforce the positive aspects of your day, to bolster your confidence as a leader. The message of well-being—in mind, body, and spirit—is a priority for a balanced lifestyle.

Finally, I want to share some of the attributes of a leader that will benefit you now and into the future. With that in mind, I want you to focus on identifying your strengths within this list. Can you maximize those strengths? Are the areas, where you might be less strong, ones that you can improve, or is there someone on your team who has exhibited those qualities or attributes? A team is at its best when everyone contributes different attributes, thus covering over weaknesses with the strengths of the team as a whole.

Attributes of a Leader

1. Knowing who you are and what you stand for, and being self-confident and knowledgeable.
2. Having a pleasing and respectful persona.
3. Having visionary and forward thinking, short and long-term views, and weighing feasibility and risk assessing individually or with help of managers and project teams.
4. Having self-control and being able to openly share your values, forming an environment of trust and certainty.
5. Being accountable and teaching others to take responsibility and accountability.
6. Paying attention to detail or delegating when identifying others can do this better.
7. Leading with integrity at the centre of influence.
8. Possessing a sense of justice and fairness. (An example of King Solomon's wisdom is illustrated in an old story told over the ages, of a case between two women both claiming to be the mother of a child. The leader revealed their true feelings and relationship to the child by

suggesting cutting the baby in two, with each woman to receive half. The mother of the baby asked that the baby be given to the other woman. At least the child would be alive.)

9. Being a good listener, and being patient, sympathetic, genuine, and inspirational. Mindfully being present when you are having conversations with those you lead and coach.
10. Correcting and giving constructive feedback is done from a genuine place of helping, understanding, and love. (Yes, love in the workplace is key as it fosters a sense of belonging, community, or tribe.)
11. Being not too hard or too soft; being challenging and motivating, and instilling growth. Challenging team members in areas where they are slacking or not meeting deadlines is a key leader's attribute.
12. Delegating and encouraging teams to be creative, and coming up with new ideas and projects without fear of being blamed for mistakes. Always thinking of developing those they lead with a succession growth plan in mind.
13. Being passionate and committed to doing more when required.
14. Making a collaborative and shared effort is key for the success of businesses and communities globally, especially in unprecedented times like COVID-19, which is a disruption in all industries.

Reflect and, on a scale of 1 to 10, put a score on each of the above. Those with lower scores are your identified areas of improvement. While we all want to learn and improve, never spend so much time on your weaknesses that you ignore your strengths. Now I want to shift to another area of leadership, which is the ability to influence others beyond your teams. Along the way, I will share how the environment and power struggles within your organisation can be shifted by the use of a leader's influence.

Master Key 9

Lead and Influence with Integrity

9

We all know individuals who wield a lot of power. You read about them constantly in the newspapers or see them on television. These individuals use their power to make decisions that can impact a large number of people, including how they work and how they live. Those in power do not necessarily focus on how their decisions alter lives or potentially damage the environment, but wield their power to achieve whatever ends they desire.

Throughout coaching and assessing clients, I explore what they think about power. I ask if clients have interests and what they naturally feel drawn to. I ask them which individuals have influenced them, and who their role models are, the ones they look up to.

That is not to say that powerful people cannot use their power for good. Yet when any leader uses power alone to initiate a change, often they find it hard to make the change stick. Often, the reason is because when you simply force people to do something, and compliance typically does not last. Influence, on the other hand, is about using your strengths to convince potential stakeholders to buy into the process.

For over twenty years, I have worked in various organisations where the power of influencing played a key role in getting team buy-in. I can confess there were times I had to deal with very difficult individuals. On reflection, it may be that you have not explained it or conveyed the task at hand in a manner in which the person understands.

At its core, influence is the ability to motivate and inspire others to take action, serving as the distinguishing factor between a leader and a manager. The best leaders are those who can successfully influence up, down, and across the organisation, impacting business results by driving behavioural change.

"Death and life are in the power of the tongue,
and those who love it will eat its fruits."
Proverbs 18:21

I have been influenced positively by a lot of great leaders, including in the world of coaching. One aspect of being an influential leader is working with your team to get their buy-in, which positively impacts your productivity. However, influence can also be wielded in a negative way. Therefore, influential leaders thrive when they combine their influence with integrity.

The definition of integrity is based upon being honest and having strong moral principles. I often illustrate it as standing by your principles, whether someone is present to acknowledge it or not. Would you do that if others were around? If not, then you likely would not do it when no one is around.

I bumped into Sir Alex Ferguson and his wife in Monaco, at a hotel where my 8-year-old nephew, Josiah, at the time was staying with other young actors and actresses, with their chaperones, performing live at a theatre. The main character was being played by the amazing singer, Alexandra Burke, winner of the "New Star" in the UK.

My young nephew was performing in *The Bodyguard,* as Whitney Houston's son. Sir Alex demonstrated that a leader's character should be empathetic and understanding, on and off the field of leadership. My sister and I were standing in a que waiting for a taxi to take us to our own hotel, a fifteen-minute drive away. I noticed that Sir Alex was in front of us and greeted him, and I showed him that I was reading his book, *Leading*. He was such a gentleman and laid back, giving me an autograph and allowing my sister and me to get into his taxi, while he and his wife waited for the next one.

I was reading his book at the time, which I recommend you read if you have not done so yet. After an astonishing career—first in Scotland, and then over 27 years with Manchester United Football Club—Sir Alex Ferguson delivered *Leading,* a series of anecdotes in management and leadership, lessons he looks back on from his tenure as manager of Manchester United for 26 years, leaving the club as one of the most successful sporting clubs in the world.

Sir Alex, in 38 years of management, won 49 trophies and had helped Manchester United derail many empires, false pretenders, and threats, on and off the pitch, by building a dynasty himself at Old Trafford. There are a lot of leadership takeaway nuggets from the book. Using the tools and tips within, you can run a business and teach individuals to lead small businesses, families, or even help people in their daily routines.

Every sports team needs a coach, and the best coaches make good teams great. The same goes in business: Any company that wants to succeed in a time where technology has suffused every industry and most aspects of consumer life, and where speed and innovation are paramount, must have team coaching as part of its culture. Coaching is the best way to mould effective people into powerful teams. As a leader and coach, the most important thing a manager does is to help people be more effective and to grow and develop. The 1:1 is the best opportunity to accomplish that. People feel valued when you give them protected supervision time with genuinely being present and in the moment. Give the coachee positive feedback, which will make it easier to take feedback regarding areas that need to improve. Praise in coaching can motivate your team to continue putting their best effort forward.

In my coaching, I offer services that help individuals and teams transform their thinking, and to further understand their strengths and talents. This includes individual 1:1 coaching for aspiring managers; coaching for managers and senior executives in the private sector, local government, and non-profit; team coaching; coaching for women; confidence building; preparing for interviews; executive presence and personal branding; and coaching future leaders.

In the performance industry, actors and actresses have to be disciplined and follow the directions of film directors and their coaches. The rigorous practice and training that go with this is evident. As a leader, modelling constant practice and discipline within your own professional performance can be a great example for your team members.

Teaching Management Principles and Good Practice

When it comes to coaching and mentoring, there is a level of focusing on goals and encouraging strengths, as well as modelling behaviours or attitudes that can benefit the organisation. Yet underlying all of these is the teaching that must take place to help your team excel.

As a parent, I spent years training my children to accomplish specific tasks. When I started out, I had them help me to complete the task, usually by walking them through the steps and giving them a small part of the task to complete themselves, under my supervision. Then as they got more confident, I would assign them small tasks to complete on their own, checking up afterwards to help them improve. Eventually, they were performing to my expectations, and I could let them handle things without my supervision. I also did not have the same desire to check up with them frequently, because I knew they can handle it.

Leading in an organisation, especially for new leaders, involves a teaching process and a learning curve for your team. They are going to need to understand your expectations and standards, but you will also be learning their strengths and the best ways to challenge them to increase productivity and get the best levels of innovation and creativity. Additionally, you need to learn how to speak to them in a way that does not trigger a defensive posture, one that will end up leaving them unable to process your feedback and make meaningful changes. People generally do not want to fail. Yet if they feel that you are not clear in your instructions or guidelines, and you are not providing them the tools to be successful, then they will resent it when you offer feedback on areas where they could improve.

Part of that is your responsibility as the leader to adjust your style of communication to reflect the needs of your listeners. The other aspect is how you offer feedback. Is your immediate action to start taking their inventory, detailing every point in the day or week where they failed to meet expectations? Do you leave them feeling dejected and discouraged, because there is nothing that they can do well? Do you have team members respond immediately with excuses, instead of constructive ways to make adjustments and improve?

Notice that focusing on the negative or failures first can often lead to excuses and discouragement for your team. Now, I am not saying that you always have to sing their praises and never focus on what might need improvement. Instead, you should approach your team by highlighting what they did well. Reframe the discussion, and make it focused on helping them get better, instead of tearing them down.

One of the ways that a leader can help their team learn and grow, both personally and professionally, is by highlighting self-development throughout the coaching process. However, you might think that everyone benefits from being taught the same way, which is not the case. Every school system that focuses on teaching by one method finds themselves stymied by the reality that each of us is different, which means we process information differently. Each of us also has a way that we learn best, based on how we process information. It typically falls into three categories: visual, auditory, and tactile or kinaesthetic.

By taking into consideration each individual's learning style, you can make sure they understand your instructions in a way that makes sense to them. People's methods of learning differs, and the best leaders tap into that to maximize each individual's productivity.

After all, making assumptions about what a person understood regarding your instructions, without verification, could be detrimental to that individual's ability to carry those instructions out and meet your expectations. The individual may not only be physically challenged, but they may also have psychological challenges.

Throughout this book, I have continually drawn you, as a leader, back to focusing on individuals' strengths. A different learning style that is not aligned with yours might make it harder for you to find their strengths, but it is not impossible. Be open to learning more about how your team members process information, and then translate that knowledge into their job performance. It can often help you to find hidden strengths and talents in those around you.

Growth in any organisation starts by recognising that there is always room for improvement, as individuals and as an organisation. The culture can be one of blame or one of growth. As a leader, coach, and mentor for your team, you are in the position to decide if the environment for your team is going to be one that fosters growth or distrust.

Managing Expectations and Being Open to Coaching

Throughout the last two decades, the world has dealt with some dramatic and disruptive changes. Issues regarding how we live in harmony with the planet, technology, artificial intelligence, and economic or political upheavals have meant leaders need to move forward without a roadmap to follow. They are striking out into the future with little historical data to fall back on during this disruptive period of human history.

That being said, the younger generations in the workforce are facing a different future than baby boomers did. They are facing global challenges and global realities that will have a significant impact on lifestyles in their lifetime. When leading others, humility and integration of voices can often be key to finding the path forward. Be coachable yourself, even as you coach others to reach those that are being integrated into your team. Following guidance from others is a sign of strength.

I found out things about me that I would have never believed if you had told me about the power that is locked up within. Think about the marvellous system we have within our bodies to circulate our blood supply every 33 seconds, through hundreds of miles of passageways. It also filters out the toxins throughout our bodies to keep us healthy. In our nervous system, we have an example of one of the most complex electrical systems in the world. Think of your brain as the electronic switching station. You can change the vibration of yourself and everything around you. There are awesome powers within you as a leader. Based on what you believe about yourself, is what you become.

Let's take a moment to look at a professional career from the eyes of a millennial. Whereas past generations might work for the same organisation throughout their career, most millennial will move several times throughout their career. As I have mentioned before, the internet and artificial intelligence, among other forms of technology, have changed how we work and play. Gone are the days where people worked for an organisation just for a paycheque. Now they work for an ideal, wanting to be involved in an organisation that aligns with their belief systems.

Results are often nothing but an outward manifestation of our belief systems. We base every evaluation on our beliefs. In order to change how we evaluate and process situations as a leader, we need to be open to analysing our beliefs and making meaningful change where necessary. Remember, there is only one of you in the whole entire world. You are unique, and fearfully and wonderfully made. You are like a precious stone, a diamond. It forms deep within the Earth's crust, under conditions of intense heat and pressure. There is work and effort to uncover these beautiful diamonds, but the effort is worth it.

With that in mind, let's talk about how you can work with individuals who are also diamonds, of a different type, shape, or clarity. First, recognise that they might have unrealistic expectations for how their careers will go, and what they will achieve during their first months on the job. They might even expect to run things their own way, even in a start-up organisation.

Issues with time management might also negatively impact their ability to meet your expectations. They might struggle with the idea that they have to start at the bottom to gain competency in the skills needed for more significant positions within the organisation. Along with a lack of time management skills, they might struggle to follow guidance.

Therefore, as a leader, you need to model what you expect. If you do not follow guidance, then it is unlikely that your team will be quick to follow your guidance. Lead by example. Be open to listening to their concerns and frustrations. Hold your team accountable, but acknowledge their efforts.

Coaching and mentoring needs to focus on teaching these skills and helping your newer team members adapt. However, recognise that if they are not willing to listen, learn, and grow, then accountability might include removing them from the team. The attributes of a leader include learning about your team and fitting the right people into the necessary positions to achieve your goals. If you coach with effectiveness and are coachable yourself, then your leadership will display these attributes, thus giving your team the means to move forward successfully. As a strengths coach, I help individuals understand team dynamics, strengths, and how to capitalise this for best financial organisational outcomes.

For a free gift of attributes of great leaders, log on to www.careerleadershipcoachingtoday.com. Now let's get inspired with some amazing leaders throughout history, who dealt with their own challenges.

Master Key 10

Standing on the Shoulders of Giants

10

Throughout this journey, my goal has been to inspire you to have the self-confidence to release your inner leader. Each of the master keys focused on specific attributes that leaders need, particularly as the global economy and cultural norms are being shifted by changing technology, climate change, pandemics, and the disruptive impact of the internet and all its various platforms.

There are leaders who came before you, legends that left a legacy for us to learn from and absorb. Current leaders are building their legacy. To lead with understanding, you need to study how other leaders instigated change and changed the world. During the time I was writing this book, my book architect emailed me this quote: "Leaders focus on results. They focus on any results!" It can be easy to get wrapped up in the fact that you did not achieve your expected results, but if you focus on the fact that you did get results, you can start to see how you moved closer to your desired goal. Leaders know the importance of getting results consistently. It is in the regular pattern of action that they will find perfection.

I have read over 100 books on leadership, written by motivating and futuristic leaders. This chapter is about some of the visionaries and futuristic leaders and planners. These inspirational stories can be used for discussions in coaching sessions, to inspire creativity and change with clients and those you lead. It is a mindset (Mindset Of Excellence: Think and Grow Rich and Believe In Yourself) with undivided attention and drive to achieve results. Some of the great leaders of our time took small actions and started businesses that are impacting nations and generations to come. The following heroes are a few whose stories inspire and are disruptive. As I list some of these leaders, I want you to compare and contrast the following:

- Their net worth
- Childhood background
- Their influences
- The age they started their businesses
- What inspired them to start their business when they did

"Sincerity begins with you. The man who is sincere with others must first be sincere with himself."
– Napoleon Hill

In the current AI and internet-based business landscape, more than ever before, today's leaders need to be visionary and disruptive to achieve results. Elon Musk is a South African-born American entrepreneur and businessman, who founded X.com in 1999 (which later became PayPal), SpaceX in 2002, and Tesla Motors in 2003. Musk became a multimillionaire in his late 20s when he sold his start-up company, Zip2, to a division of Compaq Computers.

With $153.5 billion USD as his current wealth, Elon Musk predicts Tesla will manufacture 20 million electric cars a year, by 2030. In his tweet, Musk posed one caveat: Reaching a "20-million electric vehicles a year" production capacity would require "consistent, excellent execution." This will no doubt require great leadership, coaching, project management, teamwork, appreciating the importance of followership, being cognitively complex, and the ability to handle pressure. This figure is more than 50 times the 365,000 electric vehicles Tesla made in 2019. The company sold 367,500 vehicles in the same year, which was a 50 per cent increase over the previous year.

His visionary leadership was demonstrated during the COVID-19 lockdown. In October 2020, Elon Musk predicted that humans could land on Mars within the next decade. The billionaire said he is "fairly confident" that a Mars mission could happen within the next six years. Tesla's current products include electric cars, battery energy storage from home to grid scale, solar panels, and solar roof tiles, as well as other related products and services. Its share price in March 2021 was £661.75, and predictions are that the share price will continue to increase as political. His character traits are listed as "intellect, immoderation, cautiousness, emotionality, and altruism."

For parents reading this book, you hold the key to uncovering your child's strengths and talents. Your observations are essential to nurturing and investing in your child's natural interests and talents.

Note that as a child, Musk was observed by his parents as being so lost in his daydreams about inventions that his parents and doctors ordered a test to check his hearing. At about the time of his parents' divorce, when he was 10, Musk developed an interest in computers. He taught himself how to program, and when he was 12, he sold his first software program: a game he created, called Blastar.

With $180.6 billion USD wealth, Jeff Bezos has built a business based upon convenience. At age 30, Jeff Bezos created Amazon. With total revenue of $280.522 billion in 2019, Amazon is the ninth biggest company in the world. This e-commerce giant has revolutionised the way we shop, and made its founder, Jeff Bezos, the richest person in the world.

His characteristics are listed as "highly competitive, with a knack for innovation, a fan of science fiction and books, a hard-core realist, having a regret minimisation framework (which is a nerdy term for looking back in time from his future self and assessing the things he would regret the most), generous for good cause, staunch experimentalist technology striving to please his customers, and the ability to form a plan." He is reported to have constructed a rough draft for Amazon while travelling in a car with his wife. Eventually, his draft became one of the most successful internet businesses today.

Today, $106.1 billion USD is the estimated current wealth for Facebook owner Mark Zuckerberg. He is reported as coming second in the digital advertising market, after Google, in many countries, including the United States. This makes it difficult for advertisers not to take notice. Over 3.2 billion people monthly use Facebook, along with its family of apps (Facebook Messenger, Instagram, and WhatsApp).

At 19, Mark founded Facebook with his friends. His top personality traits and characteristics include "intellect, emotionality, immoderation, melancholy, and gregariousness."

With an estimated $127.3 billion USD in current wealth, William Henry Gates III, aka Bill Gates, grew up in Seattle, Washington, as part of an upper-middle-class family with his older sister, Kristianne, and younger sister, Libby. Gates is reported to have shown early signs of competitiveness when he coordinated family athletic games at their summer house on Puget Sound.

At the age of 15, Gates and Allen went into business together, developing "Traf-o-Data," a computer program that monitored traffic patterns in Seattle. Bill's childhood passion for computer technology led him to revolutionise personal computers. Through the success of his now-world-famous software company, Microsoft, Bill Gates has become one of the wealthiest philanthropists in history.

Richard Branson was born in Blackheath, London, as the son of a barrister. He attended Scaitcliffe School and later Stowe school. Suffering from dyslexia, Branson did not excel at studies. He was more interested in extracurricular activities, such as football and cricket.

At age 15, Richard Branson started his business. As a student, he gave young people a voice and challenged perceptions of youth culture, covering everything from pop culture and music to the Vietnam and Biafra wars, according to Virgin's website[3]. "While some of the issues may still be relevant today," said the site. It also shared how Virgin Galactic will transform access to space for the "benefit of life on Earth." Sir Richard Branson is worth about $4.4 billion, according to estimates by Forbes[4].

Most recently, Branson launched Virgin Voyages, his first cruise line. Despite the failures he experienced, Branson persisted and now owns droves of businesses within travel and leisure, telecoms and media, music and entertainment, financial services, and the health and wellness sectors. Under what is now known as the Virgin Group, Branson has over 70,000 employees working for his various companies in 35 countries.

He now spends most of his time at Necker Island, his British Virgin Islands retreat.

Jack Ma founded Alibaba. Although his net worth is estimated at over $50 billion USD, he started out life in humble beginnings. Born to a poor family in the eastern Chinese city of Hangzhou, Mr. Ma began his career as a teacher. Nothing indicated that he would go on to build a multi-billion-dollar company, proving that background does not matter. He bought his first computer at the age of 33, and

---

[3] https://www.virgin.com/richard-branson/student-magazine

[4] https://www.forbes.com/profile/richard-branson/#3e16103d6ff5

was surprised when no Chinese beers turned up in his first online search for "beer." He realised that for these goods to be accessible, there needed to be a marketplace for them.

With no background in computing, Mr. Ma co-founded Alibaba in his apartment, having convinced a group of friends to invest in his online marketplace. It was not the first time he had tried to get a start-up off the ground. "Alibaba was his third attempt at a company; he had two trials before," said Duncan Clark, who has written a book about Mr. Ma and is also chairman of investment consultancy BDA China. "He saw the promise of the internet quite early on, but it took a while for him to have a vehicle."

With a net-worth of $2.6 billion USD, Oprah has become a household name within the entertainment industry. Born in a small town in Mississippi, in 1954, and raised in Nashville, Tennessee, Oprah began her career in broadcasting at age 17, on the radio station WVOL. By 19, she was anchoring the news at WTFV-TV, being both the first African-American woman and the youngest person ever to do so. She ended up founding Harpo Productions and started a lifestyle movement through the Oprah Winfrey Show. Today, with her television channel, magazines, and ongoing acting career, Oprah has become a face for social change and opening up conversations on a variety of critical topics. Her stamp of approval on a book can significantly increase sales, and she has made the careers of writers and television personalities alike.

Her fierce determination to stay the course despite all the obstacles is inspiring. Even during moments of personal self-doubt, she powered through, demonstrating that it is possible to build a viable business and career, while still caring for yourself. For young women, especially those of colour, she remains a role model and inspiration.

Around the time of his death in 2011, Steven Jobs had an estimated net worth of $10.8 billion USD. Steven Jobs spent his childhood in Silicon Valley. He was the type of child who liked to stick to himself. He only did competitive swimming, and no other team sports. He attended Crittenden Middle School, but the area where the school was located was an area where poor kids were bullied.

At age 11, Steve came home and told his adoptive parents that he wanted to transfer schools, or he would never attend school again. The family agreed and moved to Los Altos, where he was enrolled to attend Cupertino Junior High.

Wow, talk of parents who are child focused and willing to listen. Steve was bullied at that school, hence the reason he decided at age 11 that he wanted to leave the school. One wonders if the teachers knew that he was being bullied.

At age 12, he saw his first computer. He was impressed with computers and knew he wanted to work with them. It was at Homestead High School, where he transferred from Cupertino Junior High, that he took his first electronics class. There, he made friends with Bill Fernandez, who also loved electronics. His interest in electronics and gadgets started early, and he would spend a lot of time in his neighbour's garage. That neighbour worked at Hewlett-Packard Company (a computer company). Steve is reported to have joined the Hewlett-Packard Explorer Club.

Steve Jobs' career with Apple Inc. started when he created it with Steve Wozniak, in 1972. At the time, Steve noticed that all the computers on sale were expensive and mainframe ones, taking entire up rooms. He and Steve designed the Apple II personal computer, which was a cheaper, much smaller, personal computer. It provided businesses a viable way to step into the computer age. After a year of this model being sold, it made a whopping US$2.7 million, as opposed to the Apple I, which required you to buy separate pieces. Making history, Apple Inc. made US$200 million in a period of three years.

For everyone who feels they do not know what they want to do in life, Steve Jobs initially did not know what he wanted to do. However, I share his story because it is important to note that despite his challenges growing up, he was driven and focused on achieving his dreams.

Before achieving a net worth of over $40 million USD, "Yes we can" Barack Hussein Obama II was born on August 4, 1961, in Hawaii. His parents, who met as students at the University of Hawaii, were Ann Dunham, a white American from Kansas, and Barack Obama Sr., a black Kenyan studying in the United States. Obama's father left the family when Obama was two and, after further studies at Harvard University, returned to Kenya, where he died in an automobile accident nineteen years later. After his parents divorced, Obama's mother married another foreign student at the University of Hawaii, Lolo Soetoro of Indonesia. From age six through ten, Obama lived with his mother and stepfather in Indonesia, where he attended Catholic and Muslim schools. "I was raised as an Indonesian child and a Hawaiian child, and as a black child and as a white child," Obama later recalled. "And so, what I benefited from is a multiplicity of cultures that all fed me."

Concerned for his education, Obama's mother sent him back to Hawaii to live with her parents, Stanley and Madelyn Dunham, to attend Hawaii's prestigious Punahou School, from fifth grade through graduation from high school. While Obama was in school, his mother divorced Soetoro, returned to Hawaii to study cultural anthropology at the university, and then went back to Indonesia to do field research. Living with his grandparents, Obama was a good but not outstanding student at Punahou. He played varsity basketball and, as he later admitted, "dabbled in drugs and alcohol," including marijuana and cocaine. As for religion, Obama later wrote, because his parents and grandparents were nonbelievers, "I was not raised in a religious household."

Obama's mother, who "to the end of her life [in 1995] would proudly proclaim herself an unreconstructed liberal," deeply admired the civil rights movement of the 1950s and 1960s and taught her son, he later wrote, that "To be black was to be the beneficiary of a great inheritance, a special destiny, glorious burdens that only we were strong enough to bear."

But, as culturally diverse as Hawaii was, its African American population was miniscule. With no father or other family members to serve as role models (his relationship with his white grandfather was difficult), Obama later reflected, "I was trying to raise myself to be a black man in America, and beyond the given of my appearance, no one around me seemed to know exactly what that meant."

Years later, he would end up in Chicago, where he met the love of his life and his partner. Michelle LaVaughn Robinson was born in Chicago, Illinois, to parents Marian and Fraser Robinson. Although Fraser's modest pay as a city-pump operator led to cramped living in their South Shore bungalow, the Robinsons were a close-knit family, with Michelle and older brother Craig pushed to excel in school. Both children skipped the second grade, and Michelle was later chosen for a gifted-student program that enabled her to take French and advanced biology courses.

Making the lengthy daily trip to attend Whitney M. Young Magnet High School, Michelle became student council treasurer and a member of the National Honor Society before graduating as class salutatorian in 1981. She then followed her brother to Princeton University, where she created a reading program for the children of the school's manual labourers. A sociology major, with a minor in African American studies, she explored the connections between the school's black alumni and their communities, in her senior thesis, graduating cum laude in 1985.

When Obama decided to run for Illinois state senator in 1996, Michelle proved to be a disciplined campaign aide by canvassing for signatures and throwing fundraising parties. However, their victory presented the family with new challenges. Following the births of daughters Malia (1998) and Sasha (2001), Michelle often had to juggle the demands of work and childrearing alone, with her husband tending to business in the state capital of Springfield. Her book *Becoming* is a must read.

Margaret Thatcher was born Hilda Roberts, in Grantham, Lincolnshire. Roberts spent her childhood in Grantham, where her father owned a tobacconist's and grocery shop. In 1938, prior to the Second World War, the Roberts family briefly gave sanctuary to a teenage Jewish girl who had escaped Nazi Germany. Thatcher matriculated at Oxford University in 1943, during the height of World War II. While there, she studied chemistry and joined the Oxford Union Conservative Association, becoming president of the organisation in 1946. After graduation, she worked as a research chemist, but her real interest was politics. In 1950, she ran for parliament in the labour-dominated constituency of Dartford, using the slogan, "Vote Right to Keep What's Left." She lost that year, and again in 1951, but she received more votes than previous Conservative Party candidates. Eventually, she would become Prime Minister of the United Kingdom, breaking that glass ceiling for women, and showing that women can serve in high-pressure leadership positions.

Think and Grow Rich author Napoleon Hill's childhood is touching. He is reported to have been born in a one-room cabin near the Appalachian town of Pound, in Southwest Virginia. His grandfather came to the United States from England and settled in southwestern Virginia in 1847. Hill's mother died when he was nine years old, and his father remarried two years later, to Martha. His book, *Think and Grow Rich,* is a must read. It will change your life forever.

Del Smith, the millionaire founder and chairman of Evergreen International Aviation, has often said, "Thank God, I was born poor; I learned how to work." Like many others who made it to the top on their own, he started out at the bottom of society's ladder.

To all parents and caregivers of children, take heed of Smith's advice. He believes that the greatest gift that can be given to a child is to teach him or her the value of work. It is a gift that can never be lost or stolen. It's a natural desire of parents to give their children material things they didn't have as children. Such generosity, however, often deprives children of the greatest gift you can give them: confidence in their ability to take care of themselves. When you make life "hard" for your children by requiring them to learn the value of work, they will have a far greater likelihood of success as adults.

With a net worth of 20 million, Bob Proctor is one of the foremost authorities in the self-development sector. As a high school dropout, Bob had a challenging life. As a young adult, he spent years pursuing his passion of looking for life's answers. He was inspired by *Think and Grow Rich,* by Napoleon Hill. At age 26, he landed a job at Nightingale-Conant, where he was mentored. Earl Nightingale himself was an author, as well as a radio personality. Earl wrote *The Strangest Secret.* Bob says that Earl helped shape him into what he became. It is a great trait, and is humble, to acknowledge the people who helped you.

Bob is best known for appearing in the film *The Secret.* Proctor is the CEO of his personal development company, Lifesuccess Productions, which he founded in 1970. He is considered one of the world's foremost renowned experts on the human mind. Bob teaches the Law of Attraction, and also owns the company, Proctor Gallagher Institute. I recommend you read his books, including:

- The Power of the Subconscious Mind
- You Were Born Rich
- The Mission in Commission
- Be a Magnet to Money
- It's Not About the Money
- Contact Capital: How to Turn Your Contacts into Cash Flow
- The Mindset of a Millionaire: Success Magnetism Collection
- The 7 Power Principles for Success

Wow! Anything is possible if you set your mind to it and back it up with consistent, focused actions.

Tony Robbins runs or is involved with more than 30 privately held businesses, which boast combined sales of over $5 billion a year, and he's great at knowing how to hire the right people. Still, before he was one of the leading gurus of self-development, Tony grew up poor and troubled. At 17, he decided to spend a week's pay on a Jim Rohn seminar. Rohn helped Robbins develop his coaching style, which made him famous by his mid-20s.

Today, Tony Robbins is reported as being one of the world's premiere "performance coaches," a job that entails selling out stadiums with life seminars that offer coaching, and serving as a sort of consultant/leader/coach to clients like billionaire investor Paul Tudor Jones, and Salesforce CEO Marc Benioff. During the COVID-19 lockdown, he held virtual summits, because a disruptive time requires disruptive thinking.

Les Brown shares, on all social media platforms and in his training, his story that he was born into poverty and abandoned as a child. He is an inspirational, impactful, motivational speaker, and is one of America's best-known and highest-paid speakers. His company, Les Brown Unlimited Inc., has made millions of dollars from the sale of motivational materials to a variety of audiences, from Fortune 500 executives to special education students and prisoners. He has been impacting masses on Club House during the COVID-19 lockdown. As a leader, Les adjusted to change and disruptive thinking, thus challenging the business landscape facing the unprecedented times of AI and internet.

He described his goal to *Ebony Magazine* as getting "a message out that will help people become uncomfortable with their mediocrity. A lot of people are content with their discontent. I want to be a catalyst to enable them to see themselves having more and achieving more." The message of hope and drawing strength from the shoulders of giants is available for everyone. You only have to Google or YouTube it. The answers are everywhere.

At age 23, TD Jakes established the Temple of Faith Church, in Montgomery. The youngest of three children, Jakes was known in his community as "the Bible boy." However, due to his slight lisp, he was told he would never preach. When Jakes was ten years old, his father developed kidney failure. Jakes and his mother cared for him until his death in 1973.

He preached his first sermon in 1976, and was officially ordained in 1979. He met his wife, Serita Ann Jamison, while guest preaching at her neighbourhood church. They married in 1980. His humble beginning was a church with 10 members, while working simultaneously at the Union Carbide to keep his ministry afloat. He holds a DMin, Master's, and BA in biblical studies. He first preached "Woman, Thou Art Loosed," a sermon addressing the pain women face. Then he launched a weekly television broadcast on the Trinity Broadcasting Network, catapulting himself into the world of televangelism. A weekly broadcast on Black Entertainment Television followed. His membership has grown to more than 30,000. Bishop Jakes founded the Metroplex Economic

Development Corporation (MEDC), and established Clay Academy for the missed "new urbanism" community. *Time Magazine* and CNN distinguished Jakes as America's best preacher. *Savoy Magazine* named him one of the "Top 100 Powers That Be." President Barack Obama asked Bishop Jakes to deliver the morning service before that historic presidential inauguration. Bishop TD Jakes is the author of more than twenty books, and a Grammy award-winning musician and director of films under a brand he owns. His family's early hardships and his personal struggles built up a faith that he felt compelled to share with others, no matter the challenges.

Winston Churchill was reportedly born two months premature on the Blenheim estate. Randolph and Jennie had married on 15 April, only seven and a half months before Winston's arrival, and there is no certainty that he was really premature. A few weeks after Winston was born, the Churchills engaged a nurse, Elizabeth Everest (c.1832–1895), to look after him. His relationship with his parents was fractured, and contact was limited. In 1882, when he started attending boarding school, Churchill struggled academically. Despite improving academically over time, excelling particularly in history, teachers also complained about his lack of punctuality and carelessness. Later, he was deemed one of the United Kingdom's most influential prime ministers, guiding the country through much of World War II and the ensuing recovery.

Warren Edward Buffett was born to his mother Leila and father Howard, a stockbroker-turned-congressman. Warren is reported to have shown an amazing aptitude for both money and business at a very early age. Associates remember his supernatural ability to mentally calculate columns of numbers, an achievement Warren still shocks industry partners with today.

Buffett tackled graduate studies with a defiance he displayed a few years earlier when getting his bachelor degree. He was finally persuaded to apply to Harvard Business School, which rejected him as "too young." Slighted, Warren then applied to Columbia, where famed investors Ben Graham and David Dodd taught—an experience that would forever change his life. Today, he is worth over $98.5 billion USD.

Looking at all these great leaders, a few things pop out. One, they did not let their circumstances dictate what they were capable of achieving. They used the challenges of their childhoods to inspire and motivate them to excel. For many of them, their vision was clear from childhood about their purpose. I enjoy reading the Bible—Proverbs, Psalms, Ecclesiastes, and the New Testament. You will be amazed at leadership principles and stories that can inspire you.

As a leader, you might have those employees who are clear on their aspirations but lack motivation to align and achieve organisational and personal goals. Having a coach or coaching conversations can challenge employees to change their mindset (Mindset Of Excellence: Think and Grow Rich and Believe In Yourself) and align themselves to business objectives for profitable outcomes.

Our lives can be shaped significantly in childhood, especially in the first six years. Experiences during this time can influence our interests, passions, proclivities, and perhaps most importantly, our personalities and temperaments. The most educational experiences of these times are not tied to our formal education, meaning our influence on our children can be greater than we ever realised.

Famously rich people are sprinkled throughout history, including Ben Franklin, Jean-Jacques Rousseau, and Johann Wolfgang von Goethe, to name just a few. In fact, during the transition from the Renaissance to modernity, some prolific thinkers and game-changing businesspeople chose to cultivate their unique strengths, weaknesses, and personalities through hard-won life lessons, as opposed to adapting to the rigidities of formal education at the expense of their time and personal freedom. The result is that they released their inner leader. What about you? Can you look at your situation and find ways to release your own inner leader? Your young self has the power to achieve your passion and capitalise on your talents and strengths. Now that you are aware of your inner leader, what were you born to do?

About the Author

Lady Doris Choto's **Top 5 CliftonStrengths themes are:**

- Learner
- Relator
- Responsibility
- Achiever
- Competition

She lives in Dorset and is currently involved in business continuity projects nationally. She serves as an accredited strength coach, speaker, author, property investor She has run retreats for leaders. Doris holds an MBA, a Master's in Social Work (DipSW), and a BA (Hons) International Busines and Economics. She is a master practitioner in neuro-linguistic programming (NLP), a mindfulness and reflective practitioner, a counsellor, and has studied psychotherapy. Doris is also a commodities trader and mentor. She is energetic, loves plant-based food, is driven, passionate, open-minded, loves travelling, learning, and is competitive. She is in the process of starting a PhD in Innovation and Entrepreneurship at a university in London. Her belief is that life is a university. It presents us with learning opportunities each day.

She helps leaders, individuals, and teams realise what they were born to excel in, with a spirit of excellence. She inspires confidence in those she works with to achieve their maximum potential and goals. How do you know? Doris promises to help you understand what you need to learn about yourself in order to uncover strengths, talents and the best in yourself, which you may not be seeing.

Her promise to you is that she will relate and learn about what your needs are, either 1:1 or in a team, and that interaction will enable you to foster a trusting relationship in order to help you have clarity of direction in achieving your individual or team goals.

Responsibility
Lady Doris commits to helping you understand your accountability, importantly to yourself, which is a key component for every individual, and more so for today's and tomorrow's leaders. She helps individuals become more aware of their—as well as that of others—accountability, responsibility, values, and ethics, to make relationship, work, business, and world environments better and safer spaces.

Achieving
Doris is driven to help you with the use of Clifton Strengths assessment tools to achieve your desired goals. The 24 hours we all have in a day are a gift that you must capitalise effectively. She helps you set goals by setting timely milestones to navigate so that you get the best results and solutions you want to achieve.

Competition
Doris's passion for excellence is driven by helping you to invest in your strengths and talents. We help you become the best of who you are in every area of your life, business, and relationships. We are here to serve.

Finally, if you have been inspired by this book, the best thing you could ever do is pass that on and be a wonderful leader, coach, and role model for others. The world needs you; continue being brilliant. Let your light shine. God bless you.

The author is available for delivering keynote presentations to appropriate audiences. For rates and availability, please contact the author directly at: www.careerleadership coachingtoday.com. To order more books, search for Career Leadership Coaching Today, on Amazon.com. Check out her website, www.dorischoto.com, to learn more about the author.

Printed in Great Britain
by Amazon

85884298R00132